BENDING REALITY

Bending Reality
How to Make the Impossible Probable

© 2021 Victoria Song

Published by Forefront Books.

Cover Design by Bruce Gore, Gore Studio Inc.
Interior Design by Bill Kersey, KerseyGraphics

ISBN: 978-1-63763-005-1 print
ISBN: 978-1-63763-006-8 e-book

BENDING REALITY

How
to Make
the
Impossible
Probable

—

VICTORIA SONG

Forefront
BOOKS

Contents

Author's Note

THANK YOU TO ALL MY TEACHERS, AND TO THEIR lineage of teachers with special thanks to Trine Bietz, NaniLea Diamond, and Genevieve Genevieve. The individual examples and concepts in this book have been gathered from hundreds of experiences, books, and teachers. My contribution is the overarching model that I have uncovered. Overlaid onto every practice, I've identified a unifying theory of two states: contraction and expansion, and the path between them.

My purpose is not to take credit for the individual concepts, many are not mine. My aim is to highlight the pattern I see across them all. I hope to show you that the power is not in the individual practices but in your own state, which is not reliant on anything or anyone but yourself.

Make the Impossible Probable

WHAT IS IT THAT YOU'RE LOOKING TO ACHIEVE? DO you want to reach your personal peak without burning out? Do you want to be a better leader? Are you looking for more fulfillment? Are you thinking about how you can leave a meaningful legacy?

I want to empower you in all these areas. I've taken the most powerful strategies for business and personal growth and fine-tuned them specifically for successful leaders, entrepreneurs, and those looking to make a positive impact on the world. You'll learn how billionaires, tech founders, and the world's most successful leaders are using these techniques to make the impossible *probable* while achieving true happiness.

Everyone I work with loves winning. They hire me to win better, faster, smarter. My clients are left-brained, analytical, and skeptical, far from your woo-woo type, and yet they've been able to tap into the full power of their consciousness to bend reality.

What do I mean by "bend reality"? All of us have a lens on reality, but like a fish that cannot see the water, we don't see our lens. We've all seen this phenomenon play out with people we know personally who truly believe their perception of reality is accurate. Maybe it's Aunt Beth who is 100 percent certain that Hell is a real place, or Cousin John who is constantly paranoid about being sick with whatever he's googled lately. Because this lens limits our perceptions, we don't see reality as it is. We see it subjectively through our level of consciousness.

Our minds require a story—a reason to wrap itself around a new concept. When we hear something for which we have no mental model (have never seen that, done that, or it goes against what we "know to be true"), our physical bodies react with dissonance, and the thought that follows is: *This isn't for me. This isn't going to help me.* The mind chooses the path of least resistance.

What I'm about to share with you will teach you how to access possibilities beyond your current lens. You will be able to achieve improbable outcomes in record time, receive the kind of creative downloads that artists, musicians and geniuses experience, and find more time and energy than you realized you had. You will even learn how to do things that *seem* "supernatural" from your current lens. Things beyond your wildest imagination. For lack of a better word, it will be nothing short of *magic*. And it won't require any leap of faith or belief on your end.

Relieved?

I have studied with Masters with "supernatural abilities" who believe it's God, Spirit, Universe, or Source behind their gifts. My clients, most of whom self-identify as atheist, agnostic, or nihilist, have been able to get the same seemingly supernatural results. It doesn't matter if you think this works because you believe in God, the matrix, quantum physics, Rehoboam, or think we're in a simulation. It will work for you just as it works for me and my clients, some of whom ponder the model of reality we're in, and others who just want results.

My job is to help solve problems the way they present them-selves to my clients who range from scientists to CEOs, artists to athletes, investors to entrepreneurs—leaders with power, platform, and influence. I choose to work only with those who I believe are steering humanity toward its highest destiny. They hire me to reach their fullest potential, and they stay with me to learn the codes to bending reality—how to access the field of infinite possibility and probability—to get what they want. I am tool and modality agnostic. I share whatever is required to get my clients results. I want to meet you *where you are*—using language that resonates—and walk you through how to bend reality step by step. I've invested all my time, money, and energy into learning these steps, which I hope will accelerate your own journey.

Here's a bit of background on my path. I graduated from Yale University, then from Harvard Business School, and was selected to the "Forbes 30 Under 30" list for venture capital investing. But the more I achieved, the emptier I felt. I looked around at my successful classmates, colleagues, clients, and friends and noticed none of us was truly happy. I was an investor sitting on the boards of fast-growing technology companies, but I realized the questions I was interested in solving went beyond their business model, to how they could achieve both epic success *and* fulfillment. I made the transition to leadership advising because the level of information I receive from this capacity is 100 times the information I received as a board member, which allows me to support more deeply from here. My business background enables me to bridge perspectives in such a way that they hardly feel the transition as they upgrade their lens on reality.

The codes to bending reality aren't something we receive from a degree, though we should. After my formal education, I completed three certifications for one-on-one leadership and team leadership, including being trained directly by Brené Brown.[1] My dynamic training continued with 24 coaches, therapists, spiritual masters, shamanic healers, and my greatest teacher, Life.

My truth-seeking journey led me on some wild adventures from sex coaching to medicine journeys. I used to go from therapist to therapist, coach to coach, spiritual master to spiritual master, book to book, program to program thinking, "I won't be fixed until I've learned all that's out there that helps and heals." I turned over every rock, and then I saw the simplicity hidden behind the complexity. This is what I teach my clients and what I'm about to share with you.

These techniques work for everyone. Through working with a broad range of highly successful people from my clients to teachers and mentors, I have derived universal truths that work for all, regardless of gender, profession, age or status. It's *simple*, but *not easy* because it goes against everything we've learned about reality. This book will help you unlearn many assumptions you may not even realize you hold. Each chapter upgrades your lens with key unlearnings, tools, and exercises until you can make the impossible *probable*.

This book is a perfect example. It came to me in five minutes on Wednesday morning. I set the intention to create my life's work during the quarantine. I wrote the summary in a text to a friend, then an hour later, all the chapters came through, and the book began to write me—200 pages in one week. If you had asked me on Tuesday what I would write a book about, I'd have said, "I'm not sure." The next day, the download came through and the book was complete. One client was struck with the inspiration for a patent he wrote in *one day* and emailed me, "What weird magic IS this. Still not sure what this is but 🚀🔥🚀🔥🚀🔥🚀🔥." Such abilities may appear supernatural to your current lens if you haven't yet realized what your consciousness is fully capable of.

Disclaimer: *This is not an escape read.* You will be challenged. You might confront feelings you didn't know you had. By the end of reading it, you will no longer be the same person who opened this book. This transformation is available to anyone who dives in with an open mind. On the other side, you will find yourself achieving more than you ever had while working less. How? You will be able to *bend reality*.

CHAPTER 1
Your First Upgrade

RIGHT NOW, I WANT YOU TO IMAGINE FEELING SCARED, sad, threatened, powerless, or helpless.

Imagine feeling unworthy, not enough, a failure, lonely, unlovable or any other thought, image, or feeling you don't like.

And tell me what that feels like in your body.

Let yourself really go there.

This is contraction.

Feel this contraction and then turn it up to 100 percent so you can really get to know it. Many clients can feel their chest tightening, shallow breathing, buzzing in their head, a hot face, tightening in the stomach or throat, heat, dry mouth, tunnel vision, and tensing muscles. Some go numb and disassociate, others are vigilant, while still others move into fetal position.

Now imagine creating from this space of contraction. How much inspiration, creativity, and possibility do you have access to from here? From this closed-off place, we tend to feel judgmental, impatient, and sure that our point of view is right. From here, we often express John Gottman's[2] Four Deadly Horsemen of criticism, contempt, defensiveness, and stonewalling. When our body is in contraction, our nervous system is overactivated, and it's easy to trigger our fight-flight-freeze response when threats to our ego identity feel like threats to our physical safety. Uncertainty creates fear of the unknown, which can quickly turn into panic. Freezing can appear as unaffected calm to an onlooker, but this disassociated state is a reaction to feeling overwhelmed.

Now I want you to imagine feeling open, trusting, fulfilled, happy, or grateful.

While in contraction, we only see problems. In expansion, we see solutions. We see opportunities.

Imagine feeling powerful, unstoppable, abundant, wise, confident, free, or any other thought, image, or feeling you like.

What does that feel like in your body?

Many clients can feel their chest open up, slower and fewer breaths, their chin up, a straighter posture, excited, alive, grounded, relaxed, solid, and strong.

This is expansion.

Feel this expansion and then turn it up to 100 percent so you can really get to know it.

Now imagine creating from this space of expansion. How much inspiration, creativity, and possibility do you have access to from here? From this open place, we tend to feel curious, trusting, optimistic, growth-oriented, playful, spontaneous, collaborative, willing to see things from another perspective. While in contraction, we only see problems. In expansion, we see solutions. We see opportunities. It's the difference between having access to a hammer versus a Swiss army knife. In contraction, our focus is on protection and safety. In expansion, our focus is on creation and connection.

Our natural state is relaxed, trusting, and open. However, beyond our awareness, many of our thoughts and feelings create contraction. Our lives, parts of our childhoods, our insecurities, lows, traumas, shame stories, limiting beliefs, fears, and stress are held as memory in the body, which is where our subconscious lives. Your mind may not remember, but your body does. Our body will seek to avoid triggering this wound in our nervous system's memory in order to keep us feeling safe. For instance, if we have a memory of being bullied and laughed at as being "dumb" in school, then anything in our present day that makes us feel dumb gets tangled up in that original contraction. This buildup continues winding up the nervous system. Most of us don't want to face the discomfort of feeling that original contraction so we stuff down each reminder and avoid situations that may bring it up. It takes more and more energy over time to hold that coiled-up contraction. The body truly does keep score.

A biochemical feedback loop[3] is created in response, and sometimes if it's triggered enough without being released, our bodies can repeat this experience even when the original stimulus is no longer there. Our body can become so familiar with this loop that it will seek out situations that perpetuate it; the body simply repeats what it has learned through repetition. Imagine the person who's constantly waiting for the other shoe to drop. Their fear always finds something to feed on.

On the other hand, our highs, activities we love, play, fun, pleasure, laughter, love, gratitude, hope, trust, living our values, feeling on mission, and freely expressing our true selves create expansion in the body.

1st CODE TO BENDING REALITY
Recognize where you are: *"Am I contracted or expanded right now?"*

You can ask yourself this question throughout the day. Each time you ask, you'll instantly get an answer. One thing I love about this is you don't need anyone or anything to tell you if you're feeling contracted or expanded. You don't need to wear a biometric device to know. You'll receive instant feedback to every thought, feeling, and action: *contraction or expansion?*

Notice how much time you spend in each state, and how long you *allow* yourself to feel either in your system. Are you creating and living more from expansion or contraction? Access to your supernatural abilities is determined by how much access you have to expansion. Your rate of expansion and its upper limits are determined by all the places you are holding any contraction.

The tools, unlearnings, and codes to bending reality all lead to expansion—the state that gives you access to the zero-point field in quantum physics—that contains infinite possibilities and probabilities. Practices that relax the nervous system, many of which you'll learn in this book, cultivate this state, which is required to bend reality.

We'll return to this in a moment. Let's dig into what causes contraction.

THE SYSTEM IS RIGGED

Let's put aside traumatic events since those are probably obvious to you. Let's even put aside insecure attachment styles: avoidant, anxious, and disorganized reactions to parents who didn't know how to read and respond to an infant's needs. Insecure attachment styles make up over 50 percent of the population. Instead, let's look at what many of us share in common.

We are raised by families who mean well and who are merely preparing us for the world "out there" to the best of their abilities. As children, we're blank slates, soaking everything up, and learning constantly, directly and indirectly. From the standpoint of evolution, we are wired to want to fit into our family. To be excluded threatens our survival. It is a matter of life and death.

How many of us turn out to be exactly like our parents? Not many, even with their best attempts to guide us to think and be like them for our own good. What happens when a child is taught to be a certain way? They learn that how they naturally are is not acceptable, not good enough, not going to cut it for the world out there. To a child's mind, they learn: "I'm loved and accepted when I do, think, and say *this*." Most of this imprinting happens before we are even seven years old.

Your parents are only doing what their parents did, and theirs before that because they want you to survive and thrive in the world. While we may push back and disagree with our caregivers, most of us fundamentally trust our families because they love us and have the best of intentions even if their impact isn't always positive. We now understand that a child's mind assumes its parents are right, healthy, and good. The alternative would be too threatening to survival. *This is the original seed that creates contraction.*

> **Here is your first unlearning:** *The moment we seek to be a certain way, think a certain way, do a certain thing, and are not comfortable just the way we are—in our own unique expression of life—we create contraction.*

This behavior continues in school, where we seek to fit in. We want to be included, liked, and accepted by our peers. It can feel very painful if we aren't.

Research shows that the mind perceives psychological pain such as bullying and rejection similar to the way it experiences physical pain.[4] We want to avoid this, so the conditioning continues. We learn how to be more like what's "normal" and less like any parts of ourselves that are different or "weird." The word "weird" is derived from *wyrd*, which means fate, fortune, and destiny. I say follow your wyrd. Everyone is unconsciously complicit in co-creating what I call 94.7—the radio station of humanity. This assimilation happens on familial, social, institutional, and cultural levels.

> The word "weird" is derived from *wyrd*, which means fate, fortune, and destiny. I say follow your wyrd.

Before our programing, we were curious, open, and filled with wonder and awe. The world felt like a beautiful, magical place. We did what we loved, and avoided—even cried and screamed to avoid—what we did not love. We played and created for our own enjoyment. No motivation was required. We freely expressed ourselves. Emotions flowed from fear to surprise to excitement *all in seconds*. Our five senses—sight, hearing, smell, taste, and touch—were firing all the time. We were connected to our feelings, to our physical sensations, and we had a curiosity for the unknown. With our beginner's mind, we were an open vessel ready to learn everything.

We learned a lot that is helpful, such as what's safe and what's not safe. We learned what's okay and what's not okay. What's good and what's bad. We learned what is important, what is acceptable, what gives us applause, what gives us approval, and what parts of us are met with disapproval.

We learned to rein in our emotions. Many of us have parents who are not emotionally literate so there was no healthy model of sharing emotions. We learned to pay attention here, not over there, get permission, do it like *this*, not like *that*, be like *this*, not like *that*. This all happened with the constant feedback from family, peers, and teachers, all preparing us for the world.

As a result of this conditioning, we make feeling okay dependent upon being, doing, thinking, and achieving in a certain way. We attempt to control ourselves, our environment, and our lives to turn out in the manner for which we were trained.

Imagine you show up to an important event and realize you're underdressed.

Do you feel contracted or expanded?

Imagine you misspeak and end up saying something you regret in front of others.

How do you feel, contracted or expanded?

Imagine that you're about to give a big presentation at work. Your promotion depends on it.

Do you feel contracted or expanded?

Can you see how easy it is to live and operate from contraction? Can you see how difficult it is, then, for you to access supernatural abilities that come out of you feeling expanded?

I know you're probably thinking, *Yeah, but what else would we do?* That's where we're headed. Let me first continue with the ways the majority of us are wired to feel contracted.

What is the message we hear out there on station 94.7 once we've left the nest? Every commercial is an attempt to sell us something. In order to convince us to buy the product or service, they sell us how we'd feel if we had that product or service.

"You'd feel beautiful if you looked like this."

"You'd feel loved if your relationship looked like this."

"You'd feel accomplished if you drove a car like this."

"You'd feel happy if you went on this vacation."

"You'd feel fulfilled if you could buy a home like this."

"You'd feel successful if you could afford this life."

We're taught that our sense of beauty, happiness, success, and fulfillment come from outside of ourselves: our achievements, our possessions, and how the world sees us. When do you know you're happy, fulfilled, beautiful, loved, or successful enough? You compare yourself. You may judge yourself or others as part of the comparison. When you compare, when you judge yourself or others, do you feel contracted or expanded?

Happy, fulfilled people don't need much to make them feel happy or fulfilled. They don't make great consumers. This is why it appears that "enlightened humans" often renounce material possessions. What has actually occurred is that they have come to understand what is behind these desires. Money does not make the world go round. You not feeling you're enough does. The world runs on you feeling inadequate. It runs on low self-esteem.

Before you say, "I don't have low self-esteem," let me elaborate. I want you to imagine the worst thing that someone could say or think about you. For many clients that ranges from "not a good person" to "doesn't have what it takes" to "being a fraud." Now I want you to consider why you would never want someone to say or think this about you. If you're honest with yourself, it's because if it were true, you fear rejection. Maybe you'd lose love or acceptance from friends or colleagues. Maybe you'd lose everything you've worked hard to build. This fear drives your thoughts, behaviors, and actions. This is why everything you do, say, and achieve becomes a matter of *what this says about you*.

My partner broke up with me. What does that say about me?

My boss fired me. What does that say about me?

I failed. What does that say about me?

I was successful. What does that say about me?

I got the job. What does that say about me?

This person wants to be with me. What does that say about me?

When our premise is we're not sure if we're good enough, worthy, or lovable just as we are, then every circumstance in life becomes proof to ourselves and others that we *are* good enough . . . or that we're not. Unconsciously, this shapes our personality and goals. We don't want to be a nobody. We want to be somebody. Proving ourselves drives our seeking and achieving.

Imagine yourself trying to prove something at work, on a date, or in a competition. Do you feel contracted or expanded?

The more successful you are, the deeper you've lived in this trap. This is what it takes to succeed in this system. Am I smart enough, good enough, do I matter, do I have anything worth contributing? This is why many of my clients who find me, no matter how accomplished they are, are often quite numb.

They say things such as:

"I have just about everything I thought I'd ever wanted, but I don't feel much."

"I don't know if there's something wrong with me, if I'll ever be happy."

"I'm not even sure if I know what truly makes me happy."

I work with some of the most successful people, and it turns out they wonder what the rest of us are wondering. Behind every attempt to do anything great, they are thinking, *Am I good enough?* And when things don't go their way, it threatens their sense of whether they are good enough.

Some clients desire to prove people wrong—family, exes or bullies. "I'll show them," they say. We all want to look in the mirror and feel good about the person looking back at us. Even the ones who say they don't care what people think and claim, "I am proving it to myself" are vulnerable to feeling inadequate. If you can't prove it to yourself, then what? And what, exactly, are you trying to prove anyway?

I've been surrounded by the most talented, intelligent, "successful in this system" people from Yale and Harvard graduates to successful entrepreneurs to billionaires. No amount of success will make you immune. As long as you are chasing, seeking *anything*—money, fame, status, success, impact, fulfillment, happiness, enlightenment—you are in contraction. Life feels zero-sum; there is never enough time or enough resources for everyone. You must beat out the competition.

Here is your second unlearning: *As soon as you relate to anything in your life as "must make this happen," you're in contraction.*

Is it impossible to create from contraction? No, of course not. But you didn't pick up this book to learn how to burn yourself out, spread yourself thin, or gain incremental efficiency or productivity. You're reading this book to discover another way: how to make quantum leaps, how to access your supernatural abilities, how to bend reality. You're reading this book to learn *how to create from expansion*.

So here's why the system is rigged. You grow up learning that who you truly are and what you truly want need to be shaped. You need to think and be a certain way to survive. Then the media and cultural messages tell you, "You're not enough until . . . (you look like this, have this much money, this much success, made a meaningful impact, have a family, can afford these vacations, live this lifestyle)." Whose measuring stick have you been using your entire life? Did you come up with it yourself or did you learn what matters from outside of you?

And good luck trying to make anything happen when you're constantly questioning if you even have what it takes. This is the ultimate rat race. It is an uphill battle that can take a lifetime, or many lifetimes, to climb. And you're set up to be pretty distracted while climbing, without time or energy for much else. Put on some sports or entertainment for a brief break and then get back to climbing.

Spoiler alert: No goal, success, or achievement cures this syndrome. All attempts at "success" in this system only deepen the groove. I've seen and experienced this first-hand and through my friends, family, and clients.

The truth is, *very few make it*. And guess what? There's no pot of gold at the end of the rainbow.

Society is designed to keep you in contraction. Its engine is designed to sustain scarcity, fear, comparison, judgment, and the sense of, "I'm not enough *until* I achieve this much money, status, beauty, education, job, family."

Start paying attention to the news and media and see if you feel contracted or expanded listening to any of it. How much fear, danger, and bad news is covered? How much "Us vs. Them" (Republican vs. Democrat, rich vs. poor, good vs. bad) is highlighted? The constant barrage of negative news keeps us conditioned to a static noise of contraction. How much seeking is encouraged in consumerism? If you feel temporarily expanded, is it because they're promising you'll feel a certain way if you do or have what they're selling?

The greatest rebellion to this system is expansion. It is your golden ticket to freedom and your wildest dreams. It offers access to the field of infinite possibilities and probabilities. The challenge is you're so conditioned to be in contraction.

Have you noticed, even in the few moments when you feel expanded because you've achieved something difficult, how easy it is to fall back into chasing the next thing? *Contraction.*

The next problem to solve? *Contraction.*

Worrying when the other shoe is going to drop? *Contraction.*

When it comes to achievements, what are we taught? Achieving hard things is impressive. It gets you applause. This leads to money, which leads to happiness and security.

You probably studied Mark Twain's novels in school, and you no doubt remember one of the more famous scenes in *The Adventures of Tom Sawyer*.

Tom Sawyer gets in trouble and as punishment his aunt makes him paint a 30-yard-long, 9-foot-high fence. Tom wants to go swimming, but he's stuck painting this fence. His friends start teasing him. All of a sudden, a light bulb goes off in Tom's head. He responds to one of the boys by saying,

"What do you mean I'm working? I reckon there ain't one boy in a thousand, maybe two thousand, that can do it the way it's got to be done." Tom sweeps his brush back and forth, steps back to note the effect, adds a touch here and there. He knows Ben is watching every move, getting more and more interested, more and more absorbed.

"Say, Tom, let *me* whitewash a little," he says.

"Ben, I'd like to, honest but Aunt Polly—well, Jim wanted to do it, but she wouldn't let him; Sid wanted to do it, and she wouldn't let Sid."

"...I'll give you the core of my apple."

Soon, more of Tom's friends want in on the fun. One by one, the boys bring Tom marbles, a kite, a dog collar, a cat with one eye, all their treasures in exchange for getting to paint the fence. If Tom hadn't run out of paint, he would have bankrupted every boy in that village.

Twain wrote, "[Tom] had discovered a great law of human action, without knowing it—namely, that in order to make a man or boy covet a thing, it is only necessary to make the thing difficult to attain."[5]

Many of us have replaced the *love* for something, the enjoyment, fun, play (all the things that *put us into expansion*) with, "Well this is really hard to get, so get to it, prove yourself. Do you have what it takes?" (*which puts us into contraction*). At Yale and Harvard, this is how I saw most of my peers choose their jobs after graduating, aiming for a position at a major investment bank or studying for a top law school.

How do you feel after you attain the "really-hard-to-get thing"? Good for a few moments? If you're lucky, the joy you receive from achieving your goal will last a few days. With every subsequent achievement, no matter how hard it was to attain, you receive diminishing returns of feeling good. You tell yourself, *Well, I should be grateful; few have made it this far. I had what it takes. I'm better than most!* And then your mind jumps to, *What's the next goal?*

Very few make it this far to notice this odd phenomenon. *I have everything I thought and was told would make me happy, but I'm not that happy. In fact, I don't feel much at all.*

What is their conclusion?

There must be something wrong with me.

Do you know how many of my clients say that even when they heard the biggest, most positive news they've ever received (becoming a billionaire, a parent, and so forth) they felt nothing? The high lasted only a few moments, and they were surprised that they didn't feel *more.*

This is why I knew I needed to write this book. To inform you that it's a trap. To win in this system leaves you exhausted, empty, numb, and believing it's just because there's something *wrong with you.*

Very few make it to the top of the mountain. Those that do realize the view maybe wasn't worth the climb. But they don't warn all those at base camp dedicating their lives to the climb. They celebrate the elite status they've achieved, their sense of accomplishment, how hard it was to attain, and remind themselves to feel grateful. They might assume there's just something wrong with them because they have wealth, success, and status, but still aren't as happy as they thought they'd be at the summit. This system thrives on the blind leading the blind.

So now you may be asking yourself, *What's the alternative? Are you asking me to let go and stop climbing? Or just fail in this system?*

"Wouldn't I just do nothing if I didn't have something to prove?"

"Won't I lose my edge?"

"If I'm not worrying about the next problem, won't I be vulnerable?"

We'll get to these illusory beliefs that come from your current lens on reality. I'll continue upgrading your lens until we get to your supernatural access.

EXERCISE: UNCOVER THE SEEDS OF YOUR CONTRACTION

What does your family fear, and what do they value? What do you believe you need to do, and whom do you need to be to deserve love? What gets you applause and approval? What is met with disapproval? What is the worst thing that someone could say or think about you?

Think about your parent's views on "who we are," "who others are," and "how life is going to go." Consider their attitudes toward themselves, you, and others. Write them in second person, "You," e.g.,

"You can't trust others."

"You're irresponsible."

"You have to suffer to achieve results."

These seeds formed the foundation of your programming, the source of your core contractions.

What parts of your personality, behaviors and goals have been shaped by these views?

CHAPTER 2

Are You Burning Fossil Fuels?

YOU MAY BE FAMILIAR WITH WHAT IT FEELS LIKE TO live in contraction. Even if you didn't recognize it before, you're now at least aware of some seeds of contraction that may be motivating you. Living in contraction is like burning fossil fuels for energy. It may motivate you in the short term, but it is not sustainable or renewable, and it poisons you and your environment. Let's look at other sources of contraction that may be driving you.

Just as we rarely pay attention to the fuel gauge on a vehicle's dashboard unless it's hovering near empty, we often don't pay attention to what is motivating us on a daily basis. Neuroscience has shown that humans operate on autopilot 95 percent of the time.[6] Sometimes we try to keep going using positive thoughts, as if consciously speaking the right words out loud or internally is enough. You can mentally tell yourself, *I can do this* all day long; however, if your body is holding feelings and memories of inadequacy, unworthiness, or any conditioned contraction, you'll be stuck.

Here is your third unlearning: *Almost all of your thoughts, actions, decisions, emotions, and behaviors come from the programming of your subconscious.*

In the busyness of daily life, it's very easy to force our emotions aside so we can get things done. The feelings are still there, lurking in your subconscious, and just like that fuel gauge hovering near empty; ignoring them for too long has consequences. At best, you won't be able to get where you want to go.

THE POWER OF EMOTIONS

The most untapped power you have lies in your emotions. Until you get your mind, emotions, and body—your subconscious—aligned, you won't be able to bend reality.

Let's look at four emotions that trigger contraction and can keep you stuck there.

Fear

Fear is a powerful motivator. We're all driven to varying degrees by fear, depending on how much conditioning we've had around how we need to act to be accepted and safe.

Fear can be direct, such as getting hit, yelled at, or punished for certain behaviors, or it can be fear of standing out and being laughed at or bullied, any sense of impending danger. Remember, all contraction leaves an imprint on your nervous system. You will avoid negative experiences from happening to you again. You don't want to feel unsafe. That's good, healthy evolution!

When you are in fear, the reptilian part of your brain is activated and you go into survival mode. If you tend to live in contraction, your nervous system cannot tolerate fear without jumping to panic. In this fight-flight-freeze state, any uncertainty feels incredibly unsafe. Your field of possibility narrows, along with your perceived options.

You may turn to binary thinking: right or wrong, success or failure, good or bad, option A or option B, all or nothing, always or never generalizations. Black-and-white thinking, jumping to conclusions and labeling are ways your mind attempts to conveniently put things into boxes that give you a false sense of certainty. When you fall into fear, you find reasons to fear all around you. Richard Rudd, the creator of Gene Keys (based on an ancient Chinese text called I Ching from the late 9th century BC), states, "Fear creates a very effective biofeedback loop that ensures its own survival. It's really very clever when you think about it—fear is afraid of itself, which ensures that it never accepts itself, which ensures that it always survives . . . . Pure fear does not even have a target. Pure fear is simply a collective thought form that hangs like a grey fog across our world."[7] Not only does fear distort your reality by overstating threats, it can also lead you to act out from a defensive position.

If your body is familiar with this biochemical feedback loop, you will unconsciously seek out what confirms your worldview and that's how fears become self-fulfilling. Your perceptions become your reality. If you do not want to be easily manipulated or controlled, then watch your relationship with fear. Notice how comfortable you are with uncertainty—not knowing—and see if you can improve your relationship to accepting what arises without trying to control and predict people and circumstances. This is how the greatest leaders navigate change. Can you stay open and expansive in the unknown? *This is the source of your untapped power.*

Guilt

Guilt is another fossil fuel that may be motivating your choices. You may feel guilty for putting your needs and wants first, or be driven by what you feel you should do, be, or have. Notice when you're weighing pros and cons to a decision, and see how many reasons are tied to what you think you're *supposed* to do versus what you *want* to do. For many, we're so used to living in terms of "should" that we've lost connection to what we want. "I don't know what I want" is a common sign that someone is living according to "shoulds" and others' expectations. We may also be disconnected from our needs altogether, more readily sensing others' needs than our own. Or maybe we upset, hurt, or disappointed someone in the past and want to avoid possibly doing that again.

Imagine the parent who says, "I'm disappointed in you."

Healthy guilt shows up as awareness in response to a situation where we learn from our behaviors and choose to do better next time. Unhealthy guilt is fixating on our behavior or putting more weight on others' needs and wants than on our own, while believing that anytime we put our needs and wants first, we're acting selfishly.

Some of my clients feel guilty for enjoying themselves. I hear them say it's hard to go on vacation or do something just for them without it stirring up some sense of guilt. They have a limiting belief that it's self-indulgent or lazy. They don't want others to judge them for enjoying themselves too much. Being used to feeling guilt is another way many are accustomed to living in contraction. Allowing guilt to drive your choices can lead to a buildup of resentment toward others over time as you begin to feel exhausted and perhaps taken for granted over the sacrifices you've made.

Shame

Shame is another common fossil fuel. Brené Brown has dedicated most of her career to studying and teaching about shame. It's a hot topic. I encourage you to check out her work[8] to understand how this may be the ultimate virus. Let's put it this way, if we lived in the world of Star Wars, shame would be spewing out of Darth Vader's lightsaber to keep Luke Skywalker from his expansion. And if that didn't work, he'd serve up an unhealthy dose of fear.

Brené defines shame as the "intensely painful feeling or experience of believing that we are flawed and therefore unworthy of love and belonging—something we've experienced, done, or failed to do makes us unworthy of connection."[9]

I appreciate how she distinguishes between guilt and shame. Guilt is a focus on behavior. Shame is a focus on self—what this says about me. Guilt is "I did something bad." Shame is "I'm bad."

Notice how well you can separate the doing from the being. Can you comment on the behavior without making it about the person? For example, "That was a bad behavior" vs. "You're a bad person." Or, "The project failed" vs. "I failed."

For many, shame is so vulnerable to feel and express, it can trigger anger, and they may not be aware that what they're actually feeling is shame. Shame is so uncomfortable that the secondary emotion of anger can immediately override it to "protect" from the discomfort of feeling shame. We may then do or say something we regret later.

Anger

I notice people get quite frustrated, angry, even outraged when things don't go their way. Anger can be a tricky fossil fuel. Depending on how aware you are of your feelings, anger may be due to a sense of injustice, or it may be a secondary emotion. It may feel easier to connect to anger than sadness. For instance, if you learned that sadness equals weakness, then you may default to anger if something hurts you. It may be easier to feel and say, "I'm angry at you" than "You hurt my feelings."

It's also easier for some to feel anger than fear. For instance, you feel scared but fear feels vulnerable, so you may be more comfortable expressing it as anger. This maneuver is usually unconscious and seems commonplace with parents who may be scared for their children's safety. So when something threatening happens, they more easily communicate their outrage than their fear.

What I've noticed with some female clients is that anger can be very uncomfortable to access. Sadness is easier for them to experience than anger. When something happens to them that feels unjust, instead of getting angry and saying, "This is not okay," they often withdraw and feel sad, and more like a victim in the situation. It feels like a more acceptable and safer response than getting angry. However, like a protective mama bear, these same female clients seem to access anger more easily on behalf of someone else. Some male clients who've seen unhealthy expressions of anger demonstrated through toxic masculinity are also uncomfortable accessing their anger out of fear of expressing the harmful rage they've witnessed.

Many believe that anger is a bad emotion, to be avoided. Some clients find me specifically to work on anger. They say, "I don't know why I get so angry." It's also equally common for clients to say, "I don't really get angry. I can't remember the last time I was angry," as if this were a good thing.

There are no good vs. bad or right vs. wrong emotions.

Emotions are rich and complex and are key to learning how to remove contraction and live in expansion. As you'll soon learn, there are no good vs. bad or right vs. wrong emotions. That's another false belief that comes from your current level of consciousness.

Here is your fourth unlearning: *All emotions are simply energy-in-motion, which is why you cannot selectively numb "negative" emotions and feel only "positive" emotions.*

It is labeling an emotion as "negative" that leads to a repressive or reactive state. For instance, you may consider anger, grief, and fear "negative" and avoid feeling these emotions. Repressed anger becomes rage. Repressed grief becomes depression. Repressed fear becomes panic. If you do not allow these e-motions (energy-in-motion) to move through you, they become a stuck energy pattern in your nervous system.

If you attempt to ignore, stuff down, or avoid unpleasant emotions, they will hold power over you. You need to learn to feel them in order to release them. If you don't, then these contractive patterns will keep you wound up, tight, and easy to trigger into deeper contraction. These contractions can make you feel as if you have to control circumstances and people; it has to go the way you think it should *or else*. They keep you in scarcity, anxiety, negative self-talk, judgment, and mistrust. Contraction.

It's like being in a constant vigilant state. Can you imagine trying to do *anything* while there's a killer waiting for you right outside your door? There is no killer, and yet that's what your body is prepared for in this state. Like fossil fuels, it may work for a time, but it's not a sustainable source of motivation. Fuels based in contraction lead to burnout.

CATCH CONTRACTING BELIEFS

Like the quality fuel of a runner's diet, your mental process is a key ingredient in your fuel. Are you feeding yourself high- or low-quality thoughts? When it comes to how you see yourself, the world, and your life, are you fueling yourself with thoughts that expand or contract you? Are you believing an old story or are you writing a new one? If you do not manage the power of your mind, fear will run your life. Do not underestimate the power of your thoughts.

My clients come to me with quite a bit of contraction. All their self-talk and beliefs put them into further contraction. Here are some examples:

"I'm not where I'm supposed to be, so I beat myself up about it."

"I work harder, longer hours. I don't allow myself breaks."

"No matter what I do, it's never enough; there's another fire to put out every day."

"I can't turn off my mind. I live and breathe problem-solving."

"I can't relax until XYZ happens."

They live and operate from contraction and when they don't see the results they want, their "solutions" create even more contraction. They've internalized a bootcamp coach in every corner of their mind and in every area of their life.

How aware are you of your beliefs? Do you catch yourself in the middle of a limiting one or do you let it run unchecked? Notice how it feels in your body as you feel into the energy behind each limiting belief. Each one is a constraint, binding your energy and creating contraction. *Question them.* Just as it feels like a limit in the body, it is creating a limit on your reality. Your power comes from how quickly you can catch yourself in the middle of a limitation created by a belief.

2ⁿᵈ CODE TO BENDING REALITY
Choose your thoughts carefully.

How often do you question your beliefs? How often do you just assume all your thoughts are true and useful, and move through life on autopilot? Identify the thoughts and beliefs you hold that create contraction across every topic: love, money, power, relationships, career, leadership, health, parenting, family, body, sex, time, men, women, self, others, and how the world works.

Go through each of your contraction-creating beliefs and imagine:

"What if I didn't have this belief?

"What would be possible if I didn't carry this belief?"

"What if I actually held the *opposite* of that belief?"

Feel into that. Feel the expansion behind that new belief. What would be possible if you lived from this expansion instead?

« »

Interrupting your inner dialogue, questioning your beliefs and the narrative you tell yourself, and shifting the thoughts that create contraction is a prerequisite to becoming limitless. While mindset is important, it is only *one* piece of the puzzle, merely the tip of the iceberg. It's table stakes if you want to learn how to access your supernatural abilities. This is why there are so many mindset books out there (ironically, it's the hyper analytical part of your mind that blocks off access to the field of infinite possibility and probability). What is widely overlooked is the critical role your emotions play in determining your internal state. You will soon learn how to use every unpleasant feeling as rocket fuel for expansion. By consciously cultivating your thoughts and feelings, you will be able to take action from there.

EXERCISE: IDENTIFY BELIEFS THAT CREATE CONTRACTION

Let's explore the thoughts and beliefs that create contraction. Here is a list of statements my clients have shared with me over the years. Circle the ones you can relate to.

- What's wrong with me?
- I'm not where I'm supposed to be.
- I feel like a fraud.
- Will things work out for me?
- I'm an idiot.
- I'm an embarrassment.
- Will I mess it up?
- I'm too much.
- I'm not enough.
- Am I lovable?
- I'm too young.
- I'm too old.
- What if I'm rejected?
- I'm nobody without my accomplishments.
- I'm not doing enough.
- Does anyone really care?
- Nobody's on my team
- I'm all alone.
- What if I fail?
- I never quite feel like I belong.
- Am I safe?
- I can't count on anyone but myself.
- Am I going to be let down again?
- I have to protect myself from harm.
- I'm lost and confused.
- I don't have anything to bring to the table.
- I don't have enough time/ energy/talent.
- Am I worthy?
- I'm not important.
- I'm not good enough.
- Do I matter?
- I'm useless.
- I'm hopeless.
- When will the other shoe drop?
- I'm powerless.
- I'm selfish.
- Will I be okay?
- I'm unreliable.
- I don't have what it takes.
- I'm lazy.

- Will I be taken advantage of?
- I'm not that interesting.
- Do I deserve this?
- I'm a joke.
- I'm unoriginal.
- What if they laugh at me?
- I'm boring.
- I'm insincere.
- Am I a good person?
- Nobody would put up with me.
- I'm going to end up alone.
- Why is this happening to me?

Now create your own list. What other thoughts bring up fear, anger, shame, or guilt that are not on this list? Write them down. What does your negative self-talk sound like?

Feel into your last few days and see if you can pick out the moments you felt contracted. What was the thought? What was the feeling? And what was the sensation in your body? For example, "My kids were bored and upset. The thought I had was, *I'm a bad parent.* The feeling was *shame.* The sensation was a *bottomless pit in my stomach.*"

CHAPTER 3
How to Access Fuel for Expansion

WE'VE LOOKED AT WHAT IT'S LIKE TO LIVE IN CONTRAC-tion and be motivated by toxic fuel such as fear, guilt, or shame. Now I want to show you what it looks like to live in expansion. When you're motivated by clean energy—renewable, sustainable fuels—you expand. This is how you achieve your personal peak without burning out. We'll explore some of these in detail, and then I'm going to give you tools and techniques to work, love, and live from expansion that you can use right now to get started.

FOUR KEYS TO EXPANSION

I've attended dozens of seminars and classes to learn techniques business and life coaches use to help people. I've found there are common themes that almost every one of these trainings teach that I realized were keys that unlock expansion. You probably are not looking to this book to learn how to be a coach for others, but I'd like to share a few secrets from the "teacher's manual" with you that highlight how to access expansion.

Discover Your Purpose

One of the first things you learn in coach training, whether that's business or life coaching, is the importance of having a sense of purpose. You learn tools and exercises for helping your clients identify their mission, their calling, their *why*. This renewable, sustainable fuel empowers you to operate from expansion. A why that's big enough to inspire and pull you out of any small story, limiting belief or fear and into expansion. What is key about uncovering your mission is that you become unattached to the form it takes. Instead of becoming attached to one idea, project, or company as the expression of your mission, all of your creations and way of being become an expression of this mission.

For instance, one of my clients is committed "to helping humanity achieve harmony with nature." This has taken the form of building a company that was sold for over $2B, investing in sustainability-focused startups, creating a nonprofit, sitting on the boards of environmental organizations, and enjoying scuba diving, surfing, and studying the ocean.

Before you determine what and how you're going to do something, first connect to the why: *why* is this important, *why* does this matter, *why* do you care? With a strong why, you have access to a million hows.

If you'd like support envisioning your mission, you can find a free guided visualization on my website called *Discover Your Purpose* at www.victoriasong.me/bending-reality

Create Your Compass

The next thing every coach learns is how to help clients identify their values, their inner compass for what matters most to them. When you live according to your values, you feel aligned and congruent with who you are. Your thoughts, words, and actions become a statement of your values. Your life becomes an authentic expression of you.

Guess what? This puts you into expansion. From here, you realize it's not about which choice is right/wrong, good/bad, it's about what decision honors *your* values.

For instance, if one of my top values is courage, then I may ask myself:

"Will Decision A honor my value of courage or will Decision B?"

"In what way does this _____ (relationship, new project, challenge, commitment, opportunity) honor my top three values?"

"Which values are not honored by me saying 'Yes' to this?"

"Which values are honored by me saying 'No' to this?"

We call this values-based decision making. Once you're clear on your values, you can make choices without having to overthink things. One client struggled to figure out if she should shut down her successful international business. She felt loyal to her employees, customers, and partners. She judged herself for even thinking about moving on. She tried to suppress her true feelings because she believed she should only feel happy and grateful for her company's success. Anything short of loving it, she feared, was an expression of lazy, spoiled, entitled behavior. But she was depressed, burned out, and joyless. When she uncovered her values, it became clear that she had outgrown her original creation. She confidently made the decision to move on. Understanding her values gave her clarity on what fuels her expansion. She's begun the transition and is already feeling more energized and fulfilled as she says, "I can dream again."

When you are not honoring your values, you feel unsettled, dissonant, and disconnected from your true self. This creates contraction. From this place, your judgment, fears, insecurities, and black-and-white thinking all get loud. This is where Karpman's Drama Triangle[10] of Victim, Hero, and Villain can show up. The Drama Triangle is the way the mind tries to make meaning of contractive experiences. We tend to cast ourselves and others into these roles to feel a greater sense of control. You might feel like the Victim in a situation and cast the person who makes you feel that way as the Villain and the person who can solve the problem for you as the Hero. But thinking in terms of these one-dimensional roles keeps us from accessing the truth and complexity of our situation.

Honoring your values allows you to live according to your own measures of self-worth from the inside out, not from the outside in.

Honoring your values allows you to live according to your own measures of self-worth from the inside out, not from the outside in. To live in expansion, let your values serve as your compass. This is how you allow every choice you make to be an expression of who you are. When you consider taking on a challenge, make it an *inspiring* one, one that is connected to your values and mission, which ensures you are energized rather than drained. When you do, you access some pretty expansive fuel.

If you'd like to excavate your values, you can find a free exercise on my website called Create Your Compass at www.victoriasong.me/bending-reality

Your Zone of Genius

By following your expansion, you'll begin operating from your zone of genius, using your unique gifts and doing what feels like a 10 for *you*. What's a 10 for me will be different from what's a 10 for you. How do you know if you're operating in your zone of genius? It will feel like play for you. You'll feel creative, joyful, and energized. For example, star basketball players are in their zone of genius that gives them access to expansion, what some call "in the zone." They describe the experience of seeing the basketball hoop appear 3 times larger than usual, feeling time slow down, and finding it easy to make the shot. This flow state is available to you as well when you're doing what feels like play for you.

You know that expression of work that is so fun that you'd be willing to do it for free? Having your unique gifts economically valued feels wonderful and getting to play in your zone of genius is a dream come true. No motivation is required. My clients and I say we have our dream jobs, getting financially rewarded for doing what is fun for us while making positive contributions.

Learning here also feels fun. It's the difference between learning something in school that you *have to* learn versus studying something for fun because you enjoy it. I encourage my clients to spend all their time and energy in their zone of genius and delegate all that is not, even if they're really good at it. If you don't enjoy the thing you're really good at, outsource it. If you let non-10s put you into contraction, then you won't be coming from expansion even for your 10s. Your zone of genius will then get a watered down, exhausted, contracted version of you.

Remember when I told you that what I'm sharing with you is *simple*, but *not easy* because it goes against everything we've learned? For some of us, this is hard to believe. I have permission to play and only do what feels like a 10 for me? Yes!

Here is your fifth unlearning: *There are many things you can do, but the thing that's going to get you access to your supernatural abilities is the thing that feels like play for you because that's what gives you access to expansion.*

If you notice any intrusive thoughts or objections to this, it means your mind doesn't feel safe with what I'm sharing here. What does lack of safety do? It creates contraction. Don't override where you are right now. Trust that there will be space for this as your consciousness expands. Let's continue upgrading your lens on reality until you see just how much your consciousness is really capable of.

Love What You Do

What's the greatest state of expansion? Do what you love. You may have heard the expression, "Choose love over fear. Love is the answer." Love is one of the highest states of expansion. Fear is one of the lowest states of contraction. This is where that expression comes from, "Choose a job you love, and you'll never work a day in your life." The highest reward comes from being in complete expansion. From here, creating, navigating, and upleveling come with ease because you see opportunities and solutions everywhere. You're gliding in the stream of miracles—what appears to your current consciousness as magic.

Will you allow yourself to be motivated by love and expansion instead of fear and contraction? Will you empower yourself, your children, and your employees to be motivated by play and love? Will you create safe environments that sustain expansion, instead of breed contraction?

This is where the magic happens.

Why do entrepreneurs have to be a little crazy to believe they can succeed against the odds? Can they stay expanded through their vision, mission, values, play, and love for what they do through all the ups and downs, bruises to their ego, constant risks, and uncertainty? Can they find and operate from their zone of genius—staying in flow—what feels like play for them? Can they create from expansion, a renewable, sustainable fuel or are they struggling to create from contraction, the toxic fuel of scarcity, fear, and proving oneself. If you let contraction win, you're done. *That's all the difference.*

As a venture capital investor, I often heard people say, "This founder has a chip on their shoulder. They've got something to prove. I like that. They're hungry, a winner." What I heard was, "This person is in contraction and will make whether their company succeeds or fails a matter of life or death of their ego." That is a non-renewable, non-sustainable fossil fuel that poisons the founder and their environment. I look for founders who have an inspiring vision, a hunger for growth, drive to fulfill their mission, desire to make an impact from their zone of genius, and a love for their work. Because this is how it looks to be motivated by fuel for expansion to achieve improbable outcomes in record time.

One of my clients, Hannu Rajaniemi, co-founder and CEO of HelixNano, has become a master at living in expansion. When Hannu found me, he wasn't sure he wanted to be the CEO of his company, which was working on curing cancer. He felt drained from all that he was juggling and, no matter how much he did, he perpetually felt behind. With his inner critic loud, he was used to operating from contraction. Today Hannu will tell you that despite how much he stretches his visions to include the most epic outcomes he can possibly imagine, his actual results far exceed them. For example, HelixNano and its small six-person team had never worked on vaccines before the COVID-19 pandemic. Then in 3 months, not only did they develop a potent vaccine, they also identified a huge design flaw in existing vaccines. In March 2020, they identified the problem of the virus rapidly evolving a year ahead of everyone else and built technologies to solve it. They are on the verge of developing an evolutionary resistant vaccine that will have profound implications for all other infectious diseases and cancer.

How did this small six-person team go from knowing nothing about vaccines to creating one that's more effective than those developed by the largest pharmaceutical companies? Hannu and his team have become masters at living, creating, and operating from expansion. They're fueled by their mission, values, play, and love for their work. This enables them to stay expanded through the uncertainty of exploring difficult problems long enough to find answers that elude those who struggle to sit in the discomfort of the unknown. In contraction, it's challenging to stay in the complexity and easy to oversimplify, grab for a false sense of certainty, and converge on consensus. We need more solutions in the world that come from expansion.

EXPANSION TRAINING TOOLS

Here are a handful of expansion training tools I've collected over the years. Circle the ones you'll try this week.

- **Daily Gratitude.** What are 10 things you're grateful for today? This is the fastest ROI on your time.
- **Wish List.** "What do I want? What would I love to happen?" List as many desires as you can think of.
- **Ideal Day.** Imagine or write out how today will be your best day ever.
- **Morning Pages.** Write three pages of stream-of-consciousness first thing in the morning; brain dump all your thoughts.[11]
- **Visualization.** Imagine with all five senses your vision coming true and how it feels in your body.
- **Time Machine.** Imagine you've taken a time machine to one year from now and share all the epic things that have happened in every area of your life since you time traveled.
- **Mission Statement.** Create and speak your personal mission statement and declare it before important meetings.
- **Vision Board.** Create a collection of images of your dreams and look at it daily.
- **Positive Focus.** Write down 10 highlights from the week and double down on what's working.
- **Higher Self.** Connect to your higher self and let your inner wisdom guide you.
- **Values.** Write out your values somewhere visible as a reminder of what to invest energy into. When you're living out your values at a 10, you'll be expanded.
- **YES!** Jump up and down as if you're on a trampoline screaming, "YES! YES! YES!"
- **Hot Bath.** Take one and feel your body soften, melt, relax, and open.
- **Move Energy.** Move stuck energy patterns through breathing, movement, and sound (yoga, walking, running, biking, dancing, singing, toning, breathwork, meditation).
- **Inner Child Playdate.** Do what you loved as a kid and play with your inner child.

- **Positive Self-Talk.** Talk to yourself gently and encouragingly, the way you would speak to a best friend.
- **Flip the Script.** Take whatever thought, belief, or perception that puts you into contraction and hold the opposite as true. Perception becomes reality.
- **Write a Thank You.** Write a handwritten note thanking someone in your life and mail it.
- **Self-Care.** Do something that's just for you that makes you feel taken care of from the inside out.
- **Pleasure.** Receive pleasure, whether that's enjoying a piece of chocolate or giving yourself pleasurable touch throughout your body.
- **Beauty.** Take in a sunset, nature, flowers, sunrise, art, walk on the beach. Experience beauty.
- **Give.** Give money, time, or energy to a cause that is close to your heart or to your Uber driver, hairdresser, or stranger with advice, care, or an extra tip.
- **Celebrate.** Choose a small or big win to celebrate and truly acknowledge it and make it special.
- **Compliment.** Offer your friend, loved one, coworker, or stranger a compliment and receive their response. Notice how it doesn't cost you anything to have a positive impact.
- **Connect.** Spend time with a friend, loved one, or new acquaintance. Be present and engaged with your guard down. Feel the exchange and take them in with fresh eyes.
- **Fun.** Go have fun whatever that looks like: paintball, surfing, video games, dancing.
- **Laughter.** Watch a funny movie, a comedy act, or cute cat videos. Be silly with someone.
- **Creativity.** Make something. Plan a surprise. Draw, paint, write, cook, or bake. Express yourself.
- **Affirmations.** Write something down about yourself that if you remembered it was true then it would make such a big difference in your life. Put it somewhere visible.
- **Home.** Your home is your turbocharging station; what can you add or let go of that would feel expansive?
- **Music.** Listen to your favorite album, playlist, or artist. Enjoy and sing along!

- **Treat Yourself.** Get a nice-smelling candle, new pair of gloves, wallet, shoes, something small or big.
- **Champions.** Make a list of five people to whom you can talk about your dreams. They always make you feel amazing and supported after you connect. Reach out to them.
- **Wardrobe.** Wear clothing you feel incredible in and dress the way your Best Self would.
- **Office.** Organize and decorate your office desk and space so it feels good to you.
- **Best Self.** Dress, eat, move, walk, talk, listen, give, and act like the version of you that already has everything you want. Go work out of fancy hotel lobbies, whatever makes you feel abundant and expansive.

Everything is an opportunity to get you into expansion. When considering options, ask yourself, "What would feel *more* expansive?" Which tool are you going to try right now? Every time you do what you love, you expand. This is how you plug into your renewable energy source.

WHAT PUTS YOU INTO EXPANSION?

At any moment, you can decide to look for things that feel good and expansive. As a technology investor, I realized it doesn't matter how much time we save people or how much longer we can extend life, if we don't know how to feel good with the time and days we already have.

Here are examples of 10s for my clients over the years:
- Athletic: Biking, running, climbing, working out, playing sports
- Creative: Cooking, writing, dancing, making art, singing
- Mental: Ideating, learning, reading, conversing, solving problems
- Outdoors: Hiking, gardening, watching a sunset, swimming, sailing
- Social: Volunteering, dinner parties, family time, hanging out with friends, quality time with your romantic partner

- Soulful: Traveling, relaxing in the bath, massage, yoga, laughing

What would be on your list? What puts you into expansion? What's a 10 for you? What feels like play for you? How much time and energy do you invest into putting yourself into expansion? There are 112 waking hours in a week; what percentage of your time is spent in expansion?

Notice how your body feels when you're doing a 10. These activities reprogram your nervous system to expansion, sustaining longer and greater access to your supernatural abilities. How much time and energy will you spend doing your list of 10s this week?

50 SHADES

If the only thing you did was look for things to appreciate, you would live a fantastic life. What you focus on multiplies. By focusing on appreciation, you reprogram your mind to pay attention to what brings you joy, which propels your subconscious to continue creating joy. While feeling fear makes you guarded and closed off, gratitude opens you up to opportunity, to what's possible. What happens to people who feel open to opportunity? Opportunities always seem to find them. When people are scarcity-minded, they focus on what's wrong, what's missing, or what they're afraid will happen. They find what they're looking for. This lens also keeps them from acknowledging positive things because it feels too jolting, too stark of a contrast from the fear they're used to living in. They're waiting for the other shoe to drop. This state of worrying leaves no room for expansion.

Do you judge yourself by saying, *"I should be more ___ (disciplined, efficient, articulate, creative, outgoing, thin)"*? Do you compare what you have with what others have? *"I want that, not this."* Do you even deflect goodness?[12] *"Yes that is working, but ___ is still missing."* Are you chasing by focusing on what you do not have (this creates contraction) or are you receiving by focusing on what you do have (this creates expansion)? This is one of the most common modes of contraction clients are in when they find me. No amount of success or achievement matters if you can't feel gratitude.

We learn, understand, and appreciate through contrast. We cannot experience something without also knowing its absence. When life brings us something that creates contraction, the contrast helps us fine-tune what we want. When we see something that others have that we want, we can appreciate that it's showing us what's possible. In contraction, we tend to see things as binary, either good or bad. If things don't turn out the way we expect, we think life would've been better if it went another way. There's a lot of "could've/should've/would've been better" dwelling. Not only is this contractive, but it's also not accurate. There are pros and cons to *every* event, circumstance, and situation. In contraction, it feels like cognitive dissonance to hold the positives and negatives in our memory. This creates black-and-white narratives that can get us stuck in guilt, shame, regret, blame, or a victim mentality.

In expansion, we lean into the growth, wisdom, and advantage of every situation. We see how even the most contractive events of our lives create our empathy, and what we value. These painful experiences build our character, strength, adaptability, and resilience. In contraction, we're stuck feeling, "This shouldn't be happening. I don't like this," and we live in a smaller and smaller box of what is acceptable. This is a fearful way to live. We make our happiness conditional upon life working out in a certain way. There's a fear of life not conforming to our expectations, which distorts our perception. We more easily imagine what we can lose, not what we can gain. In expansion, we are able to accept that things can work out better than our mind's best plan to control and predict life. It usually does. We also understand that sometimes unpleasant consequences can come from a pleasant event and pleasant consequences can come of an unpleasant event. Nothing is all good or all bad.

Are there any ideals, disappointments, or expectations you're holding in your awareness today? By truly seeing the balance of positives and negatives, you remove the charge. List every pro and con—intended, unintended, direct, and indirect—until you see as many benefits as costs. This is not to say that there are no hurtful events or behaviors that bring you pain. This is about not letting your one-sided memory create a fantasy that calcifies the pain. Neutralizing the charge does not only apply to painful memories, it's also about neutralizing the people and situations we place on a pedestal. Nothing is all pros or all cons. The world is not black and white. Observe the tradeoffs. Staying open to life in all its expressions relaxes the ego, our nervous system, and keeps us in expansion, the state from which we *bend reality*.

EXERCISE: OWN YOUR STORY

Think of your lowest low, most challenging hardship, greatest loss, pain, or disappointment. Was it losing a loved one? Receiving a difficult health diagnosis? Physical or emotional trauma?

Feel into the loss, its consequences, the hurt. Now list all the unintended, direct, and indirect positives that came from this experience. How did you grow? What did you learn to value? How did it change you? How did it shape what you care about? What strengths did you discover? What awareness did it bring you? What did it catalyze in your life? You choose the meaning events have in your life. You choose what something teaches you.

CHAPTER 4
From Lead to Gold: The Alchemy of Expansion

WE HAVE LEARNED DIRECTLY AND INDIRECTLY TO avoid our emotions. We've learned they're annoying distractions and not to trust them. People are uncomfortable feeling; however, emotions are the lead, the raw material, that you turn into the gold of expansion. Emotions unlock your access to the field of infinite possibilities and probabilities. Recall your access to your supernatural abilities is determined by how much access you have to expansion. Your rate of expansion is equal to the rate at which you're releasing contractions. But remember how easy it is for us to live in contraction and barely touch expansion, before we rubberband back to contraction? How can we remove contraction? A central aspect of releasing contraction is learning how to process your emotions.

Emotions are heavily influenced by society. We learned at an early age what is acceptable to express publicly, and sometimes even privately. We were taught gender-specific judgments around emotions. Our culture and class also shape the expectations we inherit around how we should relate to them. Here is a range of things we've learned:

The sign of maturity is an adult who can *control* their emotions.

Avoid hurt, discomfort, or anything unpleasant.

Emotions are threatening, unpredictable, scary, can hijack your rational mind, and lead to poor decisions.

Emotions are the animalistic side of our nature, unproductive and potentially harmful.

One should only feel good emotions and avoid all negative emotions.

- "Oh no, you're crying, what happened, what's *wrong*?"
- "Don't be emotional."
- "You're being inappropriate."
- "You're too sensitive."
- "You shouldn't feel that way."
- "Time to move on."
- "You must need some rest."
- "Are you *okay*?"
- "Get yourself together."
- "Is it that time of the month?"
- "Men don't cry."
- "Don't be a pussy."
- "Suck it up."
- "Be happy."
- "Move on."

Mind = logic = trustworthy = intelligence = strength = success

Emotions = irrational = not to be trusted = childish = weakness = in the way of success

Here is your sixth unlearning: *The way to remove contraction in your body is to go into the eye of the storm, and fully feel it.*

Instead of feeling afraid of emotions or judging them, feel all that arises. You will experience a glorious breakthrough when you do. When you don't, energy gets stuck and trapped inside your body. Carl Jung says, "What you resist, persists."

This is one reason I believe many artists, musicians, and geniuses struggle to thrive in a system that says, *Don't feel your emotions.* This can make them even feel crazy if they move through their emotions freely. It is precisely their ability to feel, see, and express real, multifaceted truths—sometimes ugly and scary truths—and alchemize their contractions into expansion through creating art, music, and innovation that give them access to their creative downloads. Supernatural ability does not come from talent; it comes from transforming contraction. Yet without any education on emotions, many of them may turn to drugs and other addictions to escape. Art and innovation come from transmuting contraction into expansion. Contraction holds the alchemical process within it that turns lead into gold.

> **Supernatural ability does not come from talent. It comes from transforming contraction.**

Your power, your access to supernatural abilities, is found precisely where you have the most discomfort, the most contraction. If you have experienced any trauma in your life, even if you don't have a detailed memory of it, I recommend you reach out to a professional to help titrate the experience of processing your emotions. I suggest Somatic Experiencing[13] because it's focused on releasing trauma at the physical level—the bodily experience and sensations. Your body remembers what your mind may forget.

I want to clarify: I am asking you to learn to *be with* your emotions without ignoring, repressing, suppressing, projecting, recoiling, numbing, overcoming, rationalizing, trying to fix, or change the emotion. I invite you to learn how to meet your own emotions, not take them out on someone else. Until you own your emotions, they will own you. To be with your emotions means to feel the raw energy of the emotion without your story, without judging the circumstance or the person who you identify as the source of this emotion. In fact, when you're in contraction, I suggest you do not talk, type, or text from this place unless you're explicitly reaching out asking to be supported in your emotional processing.

YOU CONTAIN MULTITUDES

There is an art to feeling your emotions. It's important to separate your emotions from your identity—who you are—by saying, "A part of me feels sad" vs. "I'm sad." "A part of me feels angry" vs. "I am angry."

We usually hold multiple parts of ourselves at the same time.

For instance, "A part of me feels scared and a part of me feels excited. A part of me feels brave and a part of me feels alive!" This is personally one of my favorite combinations of emotions. It means I'm about to do something that's going to allow me to grow beyond the person I thought I was in the best possible way. It means I'm about to push through contraction into another level of expansion! If it's been a while since I've felt this combination, then I know it's time to switch things up and find a new, inspiring challenge. Remember, inspiring challenges stretch and grow you in the direction of what matters most to you. Can you connect your challenges back to your values and mission? No matter what, you'll face challenges in life, so you may as well choose inspiring ones, which allow you to be energized by what you do.

Here are more examples:

"A part of me feels disappointed and a part of me is grateful that you told me."

"A part of me feels guilty and a part of me knows that I was doing the very best I knew how at the time."

"A part of me feels angry, a part of me feels sad, and a part of me feels scared."

"A part of me is happy for you and a part of me is worried."

"A part of me is excited and a part of me is nervous."

The first step is to acknowledge these parts. You are large. You contain multitudes! The more expanded you are, the more you can hold all these seemingly contradictory parts. You are multidimensional, *unlike the 94.7 radio station*. Empathy starts with your ability to acknowledge your own parts.

The key to expansion is learning to fully accept all these parts: the parts that are scared, the parts that are brave, the parts you celebrate, the parts you hide, the parts that follow through, the parts that don't, the parts that are angry, the parts that are joyful, the parts that are sad, the parts that play small, the parts that play big—*all your parts*. Notice what parts you've made good vs. bad, right vs. wrong, what parts hold shame vs. blame. Integrate all of your parts.

Once you stop showing yourself conditional acceptance and relax the "I have to ____ or else I'll judge myself as _____," and instead operate from "I am enough as is," watch how much faster you can move, and the greater impact you can make. Say to yourself, "If you don't make this happen, I still accept/love/value you." "Even if you don't succeed at _____, you'll be okay." Watch how much more successful you'll be when you come from here. Once you see yourself as worthy and whole without your achievements, you'll become unstoppable. You'll be going after all your dreams from expansion with supernatural abilities and access to infinite possibilities and probabilities. Only *you* can give yourself this freedom, not a parent, partner, mentor, lover, or friend. As you accept your feelings of contraction, they dissolve. Only you can set yourself free.

Jing Gao, founder of Fly by Jing Inc., discovered this when she joined a group leadership program I held during the first COVID quarantine. At that time, she called herself Jenny, the name she had gone by for over 25 years. At the start of her journey, she identified places of contraction and began feeling her emotions: her grief, her anger, her fear, all of it. On our first call, I took her through a process of feeling the raw energy behind these emotions—the sensations in her body—tracking and releasing contraction to relax her nervous system. She noticed tightness in her chest and then she realized she didn't feel safe in her body. Tears came. She felt disconnected from herself as if she had been hiding behind a shield. The emotions she experienced were scared, confused, and sad. She was used to repressing these scared, confused, sad parts of herself. Emotion by emotion, sensation by sensation, she felt everything that arose fully, until the contraction dissipated.

With her nervous system unraveled and expanded, she was struck with this insight: "I have been hiding behind Jenny to fit in my whole life when the real me, Jing, feels too raw and real." In that moment, she decided to reclaim her name. When she hung up the phone, she changed her name with her friends, across all her social media channels, email, everywhere. During the quarantine, she hit record sales. In April, she increased revenue 360 percent over March and by November 2020 her company had grown 1,000 percent over the previous year. Jing made a quantum leap the moment she released the bound-up energy pattern held in hiding behind Jenny all those years. She turned lead into gold the moment she released contraction by fully feeling it.

What is a current situation or circumstance you'd like to change in your life? What do you believe to be true about yourself and what belief system do you have in place that's creating this circumstance? What are you doing, saying or not doing or not saying that is perpetuating this situation? Nothing is happening *to* you. Let yourself feel what this circumstance stirs up. After feeling it fully, what is the insight? In what direction is this experience asking you to grow?

Your external reality is a direct reflection of your internal state: thoughts, emotions, beliefs, your sense of identity, and your worldview. Once you shift your internal state, everything around you will transform to match. What does your external world show is going on for you internally? If you don't like your external reality, feel the contraction completely so you can move through it into expansion and watch how everything that lights you up multiplies.

WHAT IS HOLDING YOU BACK?

Know that because going into the eye of the storm and fully feeling your emotions rather than trying to suppress them is *major* unlearning, you may encounter instinctual resistance. Let's look at a few common questions I hear from clients.

1. What if I get stuck in an emotion and can't get out of it?

Emotions are simply energy patterns in the body. Suffering comes from not feeling what is there to be felt. Suffering is the avoidance of what is, which creates contraction. Suppressing an emotion is what gets you stuck. Feeling it completely moves it through you.

> **Here is your seventh unlearning:** *If you don't feel your emotions, then the energy patterns get stuck and metastasize, creating dis-ease in the body, which becomes disease.*

When we are present to feeling whatever arises, moment to moment, we are in expansion. We let all the energy patterns flow through us. My clients are often surprised that once they allow themselves to fully feel what's there, it shifts until it transmutes into peace, calm, bliss: expansion. And it's an immediate feedback loop, in minutes and usually seconds. It's like springboarding off contraction into expansion.

We're taught to be afraid of our emotions, especially ones we label "negative," and we'd rather avoid, ignore, change, suppress, deny, escape, numb, manage, minimize, or do just about *anything* else but feel it—all the ways we cut ourselves off from expansion. And remain trapped in contraction.

2. Why can't I just choose to be happy instead of feeling a "negative emotion"?

"Choosing happiness" by not allowing yourself to feel what's really there is not happiness. That's suffering. You cannot selectively numb your emotions because they're all energy patterns. If you choose not to feel unpleasant emotions, you also numb yourself to pleasant emotions. That's why when my clients find me, they are often numb and living in their heads, with very little connection to sensations in their body. Their lives feel dull, their life force is subdued, and they can't figure out what's missing. They don't realize that by disconnecting from *any* emotion, they block themselves from *all* emotions.

Imagine being born with access to a castle with infinite rooms all filled with the diversity of life, and then because you don't want to feel certain emotions, you control, predict, and manage life, people, and circumstances to the point that you only feel safe and comfortable in one room. This is what it looks like to choose to live in contraction. Your sense of safety and comfort are conditional upon things going exactly how you need them to go. This is your golden cage, a fragile existence, and a way to live in constant contraction. The goal of cultivating expansion is not to create a perfect room to live in that you have mastery over. The goal is to be able to be with whatever arises in life and still find your way to expansion. Only then can you live freely.

Choosing any emotion over the one that is right there in front of you keeps you in contraction.

Stuck energy patterns turn into moods, and then states, if they're not felt and acknowledged. This can create more resistance to experiencing emotions because you may feel like the diluted version of the emotion has already been hanging around like a cloud for a while and you've been able to "manage it." However, once you allow the emotion fully, it dissipates and you gain access to vibrant energy coursing through your body. You connect to your creativity and your sense of aliveness, the "I'M ALIVE" kind of life force. Choosing any emotion over the one that is right there in front of you keeps you in contraction. You may think you're choosing expansion by choosing "happiness," but anytime you're not feeling what's right in front of you, you create contraction.

Some of my teachers describe any avoidance of feeling what's there as an addiction—whatever you do, use, turn to, in order to avoid feeling something that you don't want to feel, is an addiction. That's right, so whether you use social media, TV, dating, work, busyness, shopping, blaming, food, socializing, alcohol, smoking, drugs, or sex to distract yourself from feeling what's there, you're creating an addiction and keeping yourself in contraction. It's not about the thing itself, but why you reach for the thing that determines if it's addiction. There are plenty of secondary markets that profit off people ignoring their emotions with drugs, alcohol, tobacco, porn, anything that supports you not wanting to feel what's present in the moment.

3. What if I don't feel much and don't notice much sensation in my body?

This is where I was, and where most of my clients are when they find me. This is partly why I've acquired so many tools for this because I was in my head and not in my body. As soon as I tried to feel an uncomfortable emotion, it would disappear or hide. I'd let it pass over me and think to myself, "I don't feel it anymore." I realized a wall was unconsciously going up as a defense. I was "protecting myself" from feeling it. My body didn't feel it would be safe allowing in the emotion. I often froze and got sleepy.

I slowly taught and trained my nervous system that it was safe to relax and feel. I'll share more of the tools and techniques I learned with you so you can do the same.

HOW SAFE DOES YOUR NERVOUS SYSTEM FEEL?

The amount of uncertainty, risk, and emotional exposure we can be with is dictated by how much safety we feel in our nervous system.

One of my teachers, NaniLea Diamond,[14] asks, "Can you lean in and feel what's underneath the discomfort?" Can you be with *all of life* or only with the parts of it you can control? Do you filter your emotions and hide behind your busy work schedule, relationships and responsibilities? It's almost impossible to sit in uncertainty if you don't feel safe. Where do you source your safety? Certainty? Control? Logic? Trust? Faith? Vision? Mission? Love?

Your nervous system's bandwidth determines what emotions you are willing to feel, what perspectives you have access to, and how much reality you can handle. Life is filled with uncertainty. The question is, how ready is your nervous system to deal with life? Your quality of life and your health are in direct proportion to the amount of uncertainty your nervous system can handle. A tight nervous system holding patterns of contraction struggles to sit in any uncertainty. Any loss of control or not knowing creates immense stress and anxiety for this type of nervous system. On the other hand, a relaxed and expanded nervous system can sit in the discomfort of the unknown. This type of nervous system can more accurately see and handle reality.

Processing feelings and sensations—releasing the tightening of the nervous system—increases your bandwidth to take in more information. By opening up your nervous system, you're able to access all the information from your subconscious including new thoughts, ideas, and connections that you didn't even know existed. Each time you feel an emotion, your nervous system relaxes, and the contraction is released. You upgrade your lens on reality with each unraveling of the nervous system.

It took me years to get to a place where my emotions flow through me like ocean waves. Every time I cry, scream, feel my rage, my fear, my grief, I know that I'm releasing old stories and wounds from my nervous system. I'm shaving off layers and layers each time. I release the places in my body that are holding those feelings and new awareness awakens. I then expand to be able to feel *more*. When I feel an emotion, I celebrate that my consciousness is expanded enough to receive it, that my nervous system is ready to process and release this energy.

You may feel safer feeling your emotions at 40 percent instead of letting yourself fully feel them at a 100 percent. But when you only let yourself feel them at 40 percent, you only reclaim 40 percent of your expansion. Whereas, when you let yourself feel them at 100 percent, you reclaim 100 percent of your expansion. As you build your capacity to feel it all, you build your capacity for expansion. Give any discomfort your full attention. *It is precisely where you feel the most discomfort that you can unlock the most untapped power.* Feel, embody, and release it. Make sure you're not "feeling it to get over it" because "overcoming" feelings is not allowing them, it's trying to overpower them with intellect. Be with the discomfort in order to liberate yourself.

While it's tempting to see expansion and contraction as opposite ends of a pole, expansion is not the absence of contraction; it is the state of feeling *everything* which dissolves contraction and all its polarities. Expansion is found when you stop resisting the state in which you find yourself. As you begin to experience your emotions and unwind your nervous system, you'll naturally start accepting, allowing, and opening up to your feelings instead of shutting down, withdrawing, or lashing out. Find all the places you're still contracted and then feel and release these energy patterns as you become aware of them. This is your direct path to expansion.

As your nervous system relaxes, you'll feel safe going to the most uncomfortable places, the places your previous consciousness would have avoided. In these places, you'll shatter limiting beliefs, old stories, assumptions, and perceptions. This dismantling releases contraction. When you expand, more becomes possible from this elevated consciousness and you continue this journey of reclaiming your power. Each time you find yourself back in contraction, you'll notice more and more space surrounding it, enabling more awareness and ease around releasing it. Each release of contraction and subsequent expansion leads to the next in a chain reaction that releases nervous system memory and ushers in your supernatural abilities.

FEEL VS. THINK EMOTIONS

Just as buffalo know that walking into a storm will get them out of it quicker, go right into the contraction. Your body doesn't lie. Your mind can lie, but not your body. Your mind may say, "I'm fine" and your body may feel numb to protect you from feeling it. But if you tune into your body and feel either numb or contraction, then you've got something to feel.

So few have accessed their ability to bend reality because most of the world is living in contraction. Most are living in their head and not in their body. In fact, for those who have done traditional therapy or see the value in acknowledging emotions, most of the emotional processing is still happening in the mind. At the beginning of my work with clients, they often want to discuss the story, person, circumstance, or reason they feel the way they do. They have so many thoughts about the emotion. *This is all mental processing.* I pause them in their mental story, and ask, "Can you tell me what you're feeling right now as you tell me this story?" They pause and feel into what's there. Then with each feeling, we get curious about where it is felt in the body. We take the experience out of their mind and down into their body. What is the sensation of the emotion? Without denying, judging, or even having an opinion about the sensation, they just feel it.

They may say:
- "It feels like tightness in my chest."
- "It feels like discomfort in my throat, like something's stuck."
- "My head is buzzing."
- "There's a sinking feeling in my stomach."
- "I feel butterflies in my stomach."
- "I feel all my muscles tightening like I'm preparing for a fight."
- "I feel heat coursing through my body and a shortness of breath."

They experience the raw energy behind the emotion, not the story or thought about the emotion. We go into the raw energy, turn it up, and meet it. We allow the sensation to be felt in the body fully. We relax into it. What we're doing is staying with the sensation so we can move the energy-in-motion (e-motion) through the nervous system. We follow this "white rabbit" and feel it fully at 100 percent as it shifts throughout the body. As the nervous system feels safe to embrace the feelings, more memories, images, sensations, and emotions may arise in different parts of the body.

Being present in the body, we begin to feel everything we've been distracting ourselves from. We keep tracking and feeling all that arises until it dissolves into pure awareness, a peaceful, spacious place. You may want to hurry through this processing of emotions. However, *the slower you move through them, the faster you release them.* Honor where you are. Ignoring the rate that your body requires to feel safe creates more contraction.

Ignoring the rate that your body requires to feel safe creates more contraction.

You don't need to believe anything I'm saying about emotional processing. This book is written for your own empirical testing. Direct experience is the deepest way to learn.

BARRIERS TO RELEASING CONTRACTION

One barrier to releasing contraction I've witnessed, which may seem counterintuitive, is that some people may be unconsciously attached to their contraction—it forms a part of their identity. It's part of the story of who they are and how they want the world to understand them. There's a sense of safety and comfort in the familiarity of their problems. It may appear that they're attached to feeling stuck. They may be receiving a sense of significance from being known for their struggle or a sense of pride that comes with how hard the struggle is. They may receive care from others in response to their problem. They may also be in community alongside others who share the same struggle and receive connection from maintaining the contraction.

Releasing something we feel is a part of our identity, connection, and safety can feel vulnerable.

You can ask yourself, "What would you lose if you didn't have that challenge anymore?" You may be surprised by the answer: attention, care, connection, love, a good excuse, a crutch, anonymity, status, money, purpose, certainty, sympathy, ability to blame, play small, be a victim, or the ability to offload accountability and responsibility. Who would you be without this challenge? It takes time to rewire your nervous system to the new you. Your nervous system may feel uneasy and panic because it hasn't experienced this unfamiliar territory. If you can let your old identity go, you will endlessly evolve.

Another barrier I've seen that stops clients from initially going here is this thought: "I know people who've had it far worse," as if pain or hurt is relative, and there's a finite amount of empathy to go around. As if to have compassion for yourself would take it away from the bucket of compassion available for humankind. As if you only "deserve" to feel your emotions if your pain or hurt is comparatively worse. With all the suffering out there, they think, "Do I really have any right to feel sad or sorry for myself?" They say, "Knowing how much worse things could be, I really have nothing to complain about."

There's no finite amount of empathy or compassion to go around, and you cannot meet another's emotions until you learn to meet and feel your own. This is step one of building emotional intelligence, the key to successful leadership. The *Harvard Business Review* writes, ". . . emotional intelligence accounts for nearly 90 percent of what sets higher performers apart from peers with similar technical skills and knowledge."[15]

The inability to look at our contractions is what keeps us unable and unwilling to see reality clearly, which leads to denial and distractions. The more we stuff down our contraction, the more it constricts us. The moment you experience it fully, the contraction will uncoil and you'll feel relief in your chest, a softening in your body, and a release in your nervous system as the contraction dissolves into expansion.

BARRIERS TO FEELING EXPANSION

Reprograming your nervous system to a new baseline of expansion is new, unfamiliar territory, and what's unfamiliar can feel uncomfortable. What's unfamiliar can even feel scary. How much expansion you're used to allowing determines your preexisting upper limit.

Know that it's very normal to contract after pushing through an upper limit—your body's current ceiling on expansion. It's the body's way of titrating the process of expansion. Most of my clients have not let in much pleasure, bliss, or expansion into their life when they find me. When we push past their preexisting upper limit, not only is there resistance, but there can also be momentary regression, one step forward, two steps back.

To assess your current upper limit,[16] consider how much time off you allow yourself before you feel uneasy. How much pleasure do you give yourself permission to enjoy before you deflect? How much love, adoration, or gratitude can you receive before you change the subject? How much time, money and energy do you spend on things that bring you joy? You can only increase your upper limit to the extent that you acknowledge and release your contractions. When you're

> **When you're unwilling to feel contraction, you're also limiting your access to expansion.**

unwilling to feel contraction, you're also limiting your access to expansion. Then you live in a narrow bandwidth of neutrality, not feeling much of anything.

This shows up in the person who doesn't like their job or life, so they use life as an escape from their job or use their job as an escape from their life. When you push anything away, even contraction, you create more resistance in the form of split off parts of your psyche that end up warring one another. You may think, "I don't like this part of me. I'm going to repress it, judge it, put it in the shadow, and lock it up." Your shadow is simply the lens you have on reality when you're in contraction.

If you simply felt it fully, it would resolve on its own in seconds. Repressing it feeds it more life force, draining you of energy, keeping the contraction alive and well. Feel it fully so you can increase your bandwidth to receive more sensation, life force, and information. You then see things more clearly for what they actually are, not what they appear to be. From a place of expansion, you're big enough to hold all of your parts and decide what's in the driver's seat. Mastery over all your parts is easy from a place of expansion. From contraction, you think it's a war you need to struggle to win and it can feel like a daily battle. Releasing contraction is a process of ending the war between your parts and allowing them to come together, integrated, whole.

The best thing each of us can do for those around us and for humanity at large is to start feeling our own emotions. It's good for you. It's good for everyone around you and it's good for the whole planet. It makes you more successful and it unlocks your supernatural abilities! What more motivation do you need?

EXERCISE: STOP AND FEEL

Stop right now and close your eyes. Wait until you feel something. Once you do, really feel into it; see if you can turn it up to 100 percent. What is the emotion? What is the sensation? Feel the raw energy in your body. Express it with sounds, tears, moans, groans, screams, breaths, or movement. Move the way this emotion would move. This isn't just for difficult-to-feel emotions, it's also for excitement, joy, gratitude, all of them. Jump up and down! Scream with excitement, laugh, dance, express yourself. What do you notice?

What is your current relationship to your feelings? Do you intellectualize them, ignore them, take them out on others, or something else? Do you let yourself feel the impact of events on your being? Or do you tell yourself you're fine, it wasn't a big deal. **What do you turn to instead of feeling them?** Work, alcohol, food, social media, family, entertainment, talking? Do you *numb* or *stimulate* yourself to avoid feeling them? I applaud you for being willing to tell yourself the truth here.

CHAPTER 5

Let Your Emotions
Get in the Way

EVERYONE WHO HIRES ME HAS A BRILLIANT, SHARP mind, and has doubled down on their brain. They vary on their emotional intelligence and body intelligence. Most realize they've hit diminishing returns on how much more they can get out of focusing on their minds alone.

We live in a time when we put our minds on a pedestal, and almost pride ourselves on our ability to not let our emotions "get in the way." There is no education on emotional intelligence. We're trained to stay in our head, and out of our body. We are disconnected from our emotions and we are disconnected from their sensations.

Avoiding emotions, living in our heads, and being disconnected from our bodies keep us in a state of contraction. The mind tries to think its way out of feeling. With our nervous system tight, we scan our environment for threats, and find a sense of safety in such vigilance. This stress gets trapped in the nervous system and we find it difficult to relax. Our life force gets drained as we effortfully restrict the energy patterns that become frozen in the body.

The mind wants to use logic to control its reality. It's afraid of emotions, which it considers "uncontrollable." Most of my clients show up owned by their mind. Spinning, confused, stuck—they can't see a way out. The more you grip by trying to figure it out or force something to happen, the more quickly your bandwidth narrows and slows the flow of new information. You create a form of tunnel vision. Not feeling what's there keeps you trapped in depression, repression, reactivity, confusion, delusion, escapism, exhaustion, denial, and guilt. *Contraction.* Once you *feel* the raw energy pattern, you'll find your answer. I'll show you how to do this in a moment, but first I'd like to explain the costs of not feeling.

AN OVERSTIMULATED NERVOUS SYSTEM

Think about some of the most black-and-white-minded humans you know, the ones who seem to go from 0 to 100 when you activate a hot topic. Their behavior feels compulsive. They have trouble listening, their attention spans are short, and they quickly interrupt to correct you. They take their opinions seriously and any judgments personally. Such individuals do not feel physically safe in their body.

That's what it looks like when a nervous system is wound up. This kind of nervous system is holding a lot of contraction. Matt Kahn has a great line: "Our ego is an imaginary identity of an overstimulated nervous system."[7]

Some of the signs that my client's nervous system is wound up and does not feel safe are numbness and trouble connecting to sensations in the body. It also shows up as anxiety, unrestful sleep, mental spinning, catastrophizing, impatience, not noticing injuries until they're serious, and being quick to anger or highly activated when there's perceived loss of control over a situation. They may be impulsive, rigid, stubborn, have difficulty with stillness, fall into worst case scenario plotting, get stuck in a state of confusion, and have low energy or compulsive behaviors such as OCD, ADD, ADHD, and eating disorders.

Many clients with wound-up nervous systems exhibit binary thinking and see things in either/or polarities: right/wrong, good/bad, success/failure, option A or option B. They can only see two opposing views and bring me in to help them see an elevated perspective and other possibilities.

Our emotional defense strategies are primarily developed from the ages of 7 to 14 while we navigate puberty.[18] Our mind and body are also imprinted by what we observed within our parents and our environment before age 7. What you're witnessing is an old, deeply conditioned defense mechanism that protected them from the volatile situations they felt as children.[19] What many label as psychological conditions, I consider old coping mechanisms and subconscious programming to these unpredictable childhood environments. These children become adults addicted to their own stress hormones. The body remembers what the mind forgets.

In response to unsafety, some people may be controlling, need to prove they're right, or convince you to see things their way. They may lash out and not take any responsibility for their emotions. They may be rigid and expect things to revolve around them. No matter what you say or do, they may not feel understood or heard. The best way to respond to this kind of nervous system is to listen and allow them to feel important, valued, and supported.

Another expression of a wound-up nervous system is a person who will compromise themselves, becoming people pleasers. Overattentive, they avoid conflict at any cost and often end up in dynamics with the formerly described type.

When a client tells me, "I don't know why I get so angry," or "I don't know why I keep spinning on worst case scenarios," or "I don't know why I feel so restless when I try to relax," I guide the client to unwind their nervous system by releasing stress, tension, and anxiety. I ask the client to experience their fear of uncertainty, their anger and frustration, and own these parts so they don't own my client.

This is why things that calm and soothe the nervous system are trending, such as yoga, meditation, and self-care. The way to calm an overstimulated nervous system is to move energy through the nervous system to unfurl and relax it. However, I've seen many try to use such tools to suppress their feelings, hoping to calm themselves down. They attempt to override their anger, stress, and anxiety in order to chase calm. Attempting to stuff down or gloss over feelings creates more tension in the system. One client said he tried to run, meditate, and write to make his anxiety go away but nothing was working. He then let himself experience his anxiety fully and it dissolved. You cannot just change your emotions. You must experience them first. Calm naturally arises from allowing the emotions, which releases them from your body.

An overstimulated nervous system creates a noisy mind and a guarded heart.[20] The more difficult it is for you to quiet your mind, the more you'll benefit from feeling your emotions. Every time you feel your emotions, you unravel your nervous system. You shed layers of old programming and release stuck energy patterns. You remove contraction. Dissolving these layers allows your bandwidth on reality—your consciousness—to expand. How open you are to letting your emotions easily flow through you is a proxy for how open and expanded you are. You make your nervous system antifragile—more resilient, adaptable, strong, and healthy—when you feel your emotions fully.

You cannot just change your emotions. You must experience them first.

When your nervous system is tight, the body registers it as unsafe to feel. Patterns of contraction keep you from feeling emotions in their entirety. Your nervous system is intelligent and will usually not allow you to feel anything that you're not ready to handle. This is a form of protection. If the memory or emotion is too much for how wound up the nervous system is, it will remain in the subconscious, processed in dreams, and unconsciously in interactions with others, becoming the guardrails for your personality. The body will try to avoid an energy surge that could cause a blown fuse.

As your nervous system unravels, you will begin to have more connection to your body, and along with it, sensations and emotions.

As the nervous system continues to relax, you get more and more access to your emotions, sensations in the body, and your aliveness. When you experience your emotions, you metabolize them.

3rd CODE TO BENDING REALITY
Feel whatever arises.

This is the key code to bending reality. The subconscious needs to be cleared of its contractions in order to access the zero-point field, which gives rise to physical reality. I know that of everything in this book, you'll probably experience the most resistance to this code. This is normal and why most everyone you know lives in contraction. Even experts in self-development usually skip over this and focus only on making your mind stronger by managing its limiting beliefs. But this merely scratches the surface. To bend reality, you need to align your thoughts, feelings, and actions. You need your conscious and subconscious mind-body congruent. This is why you cannot rely on your mind alone. Any contraction in the physical body will subconsciously counteract your best intentions.

You're not going to want to do it, but feeling your emotions will give you access to your supernatural abilities. *I dare you to try it.* Take a walk outside, find some privacy in your car, or sit in your office phone booth. The CEOs I work with say they feel clear, energized, and creative after they experience their feelings. Even releasing tears leads to bliss and new solutions. Until you've felt any places of contraction, it's frozen in the body. Allow the contraction, find it in your body, and feel it fully. What you're feeling is releasing. You don't even need to know why you feel the way you do. Feeling the raw energy is sufficient. By doing so, you release the physical, mental and emotional patterns of contraction that influenced you. This frees up that contracted energy to be used for more useful activities than holding onto contractions.

BENEFITS TO FEELING

If you're still feeling any resistance to this unlearning, know that this is one major reason you haven't seen a bunch of people with supernatural abilities. This is a huge thing to rewire. Each time you feel what arises, the experience becomes less foreign. Like I've said, it is *simple* but *not easy* because it goes against everything we've learned. Your mind wants to control hurt and insecurity. However, you are absolutely capable of *being with* your hurt and insecurity. When you start feeling the discomfort, it's common to feel scared as if it may be too much, or it may consume you. The more reps you give your nervous system of going there, the healthier you become, and the easier it gets. If you've experienced physical or emotional trauma, process with a trained professional.

When you repress your emotions, your body is impacted. If you do not feel and release your contractions, your health will suffer. We're now understanding how physical and mental health correlate with anxiety, stress, contraction. For instance, when cortisol and insulin levels change, we crave fatty foods and are more likely to eat poorly. When contracted, we also sleep poorly. We understand the role of inflammation in heart disease, diabetes, cancer, and potentially all chronic diseases. Dr. Robert Lustig,[21] a neuroendocrinologist, Professor of Pediatrics at the University of California, San Francisco says that prolonged stress leads to hyper physiological levels of cortisol, which impacts regulation of the inflammatory response. Inflammation becomes a response to stress. "Every chronic disease we know of is exacerbated by stress."[22]

Sheila Heen,[23] one of the authors of *Difficult Conversations*, shares that the traditional Western view is that there is objective and emotional, rational and irrational. Neuroscience is learning that these things are intertwined. "How you feel changes how you think, and how you think changes how you feel .... Your intuition tells you information faster than your rational brain can figure out logically,"[24] she says. Many of us do not value our feelings as cues and so we're often left in the dark about what's really going on.

Objective decision-making does not exist. To make any decision, you need to be in touch with your emotions. This was demonstrated by research[25] on split-brain patients from a congenital defect or an accident. In these patients, the part of the brain that processes emotion is severed from the prefrontal cortex that governs executive function. Researchers thought split-brain patients would be perfect decision-makers, able to make objective decisions.

Sheila Heen shares, "What they found is that these people can't make decisions. When asking them when they want to come into the lab, they have no idea. They can recite their schedule, but they have no instincts about it being a busy day or inconvenient, no preferences at all. What people care about, worry about, are on board with, their risk tolerance—are all related to emotions." EQ trumps IQ in the long-term. This is why the leaders I work with choose to develop their emotional intelligence and their body intelligence. Feelings and sensations occur in the body. When clients begin

You can only experience emotional empathy to the degree that you can be with your own emotions.

this work, the most common response to "What are you feeling?" is "I think ...." or "I feel like that was the wrong call." Feelings are not thoughts or opinions. I start by asking, "What is the emotion? What sensation do you notice? Feel that fully."

Many of these leaders also want to improve their empathy; however, you can only experience emotional empathy to the degree that you can be with your own emotions. By experiencing your own emotions, you can tune into what others are feeling. Ninety-three percent of communication is nonverbal,[26] your emotions are sending out signals all the time whether or not you are aware of it.

In my work, I notice how often clients struggle with having difficult conversations, giving and receiving feedback, and dealing with setbacks. All these skills require emotional intelligence.

If you want to master the art of contraction and expansion, you must first become skilled with your own emotions.

HOW DO YOU FEEL WHAT'S THERE?

When you find yourself replaying a scenario, catastrophizing, or obsessing about what you could've done differently, stop and feel. Feeling it unravels your nervous system into expansion, giving you access to new perspectives, information, and solutions.

First, relax your body. You can do this sitting or lying down. Take slow breaths in through your nose, letting your stomach rise with each breath in, and fall with each breath out. The key to a full breath is to exhale completely. Take the slowest breaths you've ever taken. Great, now *slow it down even more.* As you continue deep belly breathing, bring your awareness to your toes. Can you relax your toes? Then to your feet and ankles, can you relax them even more? Then bring your awareness slowly to your calves, knees, and thighs, can you relax them even more? Then slowly bring your awareness to your hips and perineum, can you relax them more? Bring your awareness to your stomach, feel it soften as you relax more deeply into your breath. Continue bringing awareness and deeper relaxation to your solar plexus, chest, back, shoulders, neck, jaw, and forehead. Getting your body into this state of deep relaxation is the foundation for accessing expansion.

Notice where you're holding any tension, and see if you can breathe into those places. Can you let go of the push energy that clenches your body? Where can you relax *even more*? Feel yourself melt into the floor or chair beneath you. Scan your body. Be aware of what you're experiencing—what sensations occur in your body? Do not interpret, judge, or even have an opinion about what you're feeling. You do not need to understand it. Don't try to rationalize, control, fix it, or figure it out. *Just feel it.* Your mind will want to label the experience; come back into your body. Go to where the discomfort is the worst, acknowledge it and turn it up to 100 percent. Allow it. Meet it with your body. Relax your body around the discomfort. Breathe into the center of it.

You know you've felt it fully when it shifts and becomes something else. The sensation may move to another part of the body. Accept and feel that fully. Continue feeling whatever arises until it dissipates. The key is to soften and relax into your emotions versus harden and overcome them. Allow, accept, and embrace them. Give them permission to be. Denying your emotions keeps them around and keeps you unconsciously avoiding people and circumstances that may remind you of your contractions. Your freedom from this silly dance comes from feeling all that arises.

It's important to get out of your head—out of the intellectual story for *why* you feel the way you do—and feel the raw energy in the body. Imagine your business partner walked away from a deal you wanted to move forward with. You're frustrated. If you weren't holding back, what would these contractions say? "How could you do that without consulting me first?!" How would they sound? "Ahhhhhh!!!!" How would they move? *Punching a pillow.* How would they feel in your body? *Burning, like fire, in your belly.* Feeling that sensation is like closing the loop on all the times the expression got cut short, was repressed, or avoided. Finally the contraction is felt, completed, and released. It's no longer held in your body. Experience the sound, movement, and sensation so you can release it.

INTO THE WILD

When something happens that you don't like, such as making the wrong call with an important decision, losing a valuable team member, or upsetting someone important to you, the first thing you need to do is fully feel the contraction. You might say:

- "I feel like an idiot."
- "I can't believe this happened."
- "It's this person's fault."
- "I feel misunderstood."
- "No matter what I do, it never seems like enough."
- "I don't have time to worry about this."
- "I don't know how to undo the damage."
- "I don't know what to do."
- "I'm pissed."
- "I'm sad."
- "I'm scared."

Your instinct may be to think, "I'm scared," and then immediately think, "But I need to get over it, and move on. I don't have time for this. I'll focus on what actions I can take and not dwell on this." Don't dismiss or skip over experiencing this emotion to try to get into expansion. If you do, you'll get some weak, fragile state of expansion because you can't ignore the energy pattern in front of you. Remember, you can say, "A part of me feels scared." What else are you feeling? Don't flip into the mind and rationalize your feeling or judge yourself for feeling it and mentally override it. You must feel the raw energy. The majority of self-development books and teachers out there bypass the contraction. A reframe or state change provides only temporary relief like taking an aspirin. The feelings inevitably come back. Until you fully acknowledge and experience them, they stay right beneath the surface unconsciously driving you. You may have the impulse to tie the feeling back to a root cause and analyze why you feel this way. While the mind may appreciate this and get a temporary dopamine hit for "figuring something out," this seldom leads to lasting change. Instead, turn discomfort into power by going straight into the eye of the storm. If you tried to take action from this place of contraction, you would be in a reactive mode, unlikely to see any solutions. Remember, in this place, you'll see problems and feel stuck in that perspective. So go into it.

Here's one example out of thousands of conversations we could have to process this contraction:

Victoria: "Where do you feel the anger?"

Client: (notices some heat and discomfort in chest area) "My chest. It's tight, it's like ... I feel a loss of control. Hard to breathe."

Victoria: "Feel the loss of control. Don't hold back. Turn it up as much as you can. Go into it fully. What do you feel now?"

Client: (feels self-protective and instinctively leans over with rounded back) "I feel scared, like something bad is going to happen."

Victoria: "Where do you feel the fear?"

Client: "It's like a sinking feeling in my stomach …."

Victoria: "Go into it and feel it fully. Intensify it. What are you aware of now?"

Client: (a memory forms, it's familiar and vivid even though it's from childhood) "I am remembering when I was bullied, and I didn't know why they were picking on me. Why me?"

Victoria: "See that image of being bullied and feel what it brings up. Let yourself go there … what do you notice now?"

Client: (feeling completely transported back to his younger self, tears start streaming) "I don't feel safe. I feel small. And I just want them to stop."

This client made the connection between his current day frustration at not getting his way with the fear he had growing up from not being able to stand up for himself, and the sadness of feeling helpless. As an adult, when he feels helpless, he gets angry. This pattern leads him to feel stressed and anxious whenever he doesn't get his way. In my experience, there are few pure business problems. There are many personal patterns that show up in how we conduct business. By going deeper, we solve tactical issues in the short term, and we also resolve the underlying patterns that solve these challenges in the long term.

How wound up the nervous system is, how severe the contraction is, and how much energy is bound up in this old memory/story/ cell tissue will determine the process, technique, and timing of the release. Sometimes it's a conversation. Sometimes it's no words and it's movement. Sometimes it's sound or breath. This is why I'm tool and modality agnostic. I move at the pace of the nervous system. This enables me to expand my client and remove contraction without triggering disbelief, resistance, or a short-circuit.

This conversation does not come easily at the beginning for most clients. Yet when you get the epic results my clients do, you commit to your growth no matter how uncomfortable. After processing the raw energy behind the emotions and being consciously present to the wisdom of what that emotion is trying to tell them, they move from reaction mode to creation mode. Their post-feeling response is neither overreactive nor underreactive. It's right-sized.

I've been working with my clients for years and every session is different. Especially after we've done the heavy lifting at the beginning of our work to identify and release contraction, we can focus on increasing the upper limits of their expansion. I support them on making expansion their new default state of being with their automatic pathways all leading to greater expansion. This state gives them access to their supernatural abilities including their ability to warp the fabric of spacetime.

Their post-feeling response is neither overreactive nor underreactive. It's right-sized.

Today when something happens that a client doesn't like, it no longer triggers them into deep states of contraction that feel like a bottomless well they're afraid to climb into because they don't know how long it'll take to climb back out.

Through our work, their nervous system remains fairly calm and open when things don't go as planned. The default questions become:

- "What did you learn?"
- "What growth is being asked of you?"
- "What muscle are you building?"
- "What is the opportunity?"
- "What do you want?"
- "What will you do next?"

They learn how to go from a state of reaction (contraction) to a state of creation (expansion). They *decide* what something teaches them. From this place of expansion, they see every circumstance as an opportunity to grow. As Oscar Wilde said, "Without order, nothing can exist. Without chaos, nothing can evolve."

They become masters at hacking the code between human experience and bending reality.

When any resistance comes up with their big plans, we look at it. My clients know how to move through their stress and anxiety and are making quantum leaps weekly as a result. They are constantly growing as they make the impossible probable.

FACING THE UNKNOWN

The very nature of entrepreneurship means you're always in unchartered territory. If you're successful, you'll regularly find yourself in midair between what is familiar and what is right beyond the horizon, what you can't yet fully see. In midair, in the unknown where the uncertainty is the greatest, the nervous system is wired to go back to its comfort zone—what it knows, what is familiar, what feels safe because it can't quite see the version of the self that's coming on the other side. To cross this chasm, you need to know how to deal with the stress and anxiety of the unknown. The more expanded your nervous system is, the more equipped you are to sit in uncertainty. If your nervous system is wound up, you're out of luck in these jumps. These leaps in midair are the life of an entrepreneur, and that's why working with them is so much fun. Every time they push through a new ceiling, that ceiling becomes their new floor. They break through new ceilings to infinity and beyond.

This realm of infinite expansion is possible for you as well. However, we are creatures of habit. Gravity maintains the status quo by keeping us safe inside the box of what we think we can have and what we already know. Our biggest dreams live right beyond the border of our comfort zone. The first certification program I took, Co-Active,[27] teaches, "When we contemplate moving forward in a big way, alarm bells sound with all the reasons this plan is stupid, dangerous, hopeless, or an otherwise ill-advised course of action. Our mind is particularly adept at taking a small piece of the truth and exaggerating it into the blanket reason for stopping, or never starting." To get to the greatest version of yourself and your biggest dreams, you must push beyond this border. Where in your life are you playing it safe?

Life will not cater to your insecurities or conditions that keep you inside your box. Life is always seeking your growth, your highest evolution. Every person and circumstance plays a role in releasing your contractions. You can trust life to give you what you *need*, not necessarily what you want because life wants you to expand beyond your perceived limitations.

EXERCISE: WHERE ARE YOU PLAYING IT SAFE IN YOUR NERVOUS SYSTEM?

What situations do you avoid? What emotions do you not want to feel, and why? What have you learned about feeling them?

If you're ready to be guided through releasing these stuck energy patterns from your nervous system, you can access a few guided techniques I use with clients for free on my website: www.victoriasong.me/bending-reality

CHAPTER 6
The Art of Feeling Your Emotions

THERE ARE MANY TOOLS FOR FULLY FEELING AND processing emotions. We can move energy through breath, movement, and sound. In this chapter, I'll share the tools and techniques that I've found to be universal and that will support you in processing your emotions no matter where you are. You'll learn how to *be with* your emotions versus throw them at someone. I'm not teaching you to yell or cry at people because you're mad or sad. I'm sharing the art of feeling your emotions.

I FEEL SCARED ... AND I LOVE THAT!

A trick I learned from Kyle Cease[28] for feeling an emotion is to say, "I feel scared, *and I love that.*" He used to be a comedian so part of this is funny to people who follow his work, but I believe the reason this is a powerful trick is because you immediately open up and expand as you allow yourself to feel something that is usually uncomfortable for you. It's like instant rewiring.

In this example, you're used to fear putting you into contraction and now you're rewiring it with expansion using the affirmation "I love that." All the parts of you that fire off when you feel scared are rewired with all the parts that fire off when you love something. What fires together, rewires together. No matter what your mind thinks, you've created a new pathway to feeling emotions you've likely historically avoided, ignored, or stifled just by adding "...and I love that!"

Try it:

- "I'm feeling angry, and I love that!"
- "I'm feeling helpless, and I love that!"
- "I'm feeling lonely, and I love that!"
- "I'm feeling shame, and I love that!"
- I'm feeling ____, and I love that!"

Notice how it takes the edge off the charge of the feeling, removes the resistance, and creates safety. You'll find it becomes easier to go into feeling this part of you fully. There's suddenly more space and it feels welcoming for all your parts. Just as in the previous exercise, follow the "white rabbit" until you can't find it anymore. What's left is calm, peace, and a good kind of empty feeling. Deeply relaxed, you're left in expansion.

This rewiring helps you teach your nervous system:

- "I'm allowed to feel angry in my body."
- "I'm allowed to feel scared in my body."
- "I'm allowed to feel alone in my body."
- "I'm allowed to feel all of it."

What emotions do you not want to feel? Let yourself feel the hopelessness, the abyss, and say, "I'm allowed to feel hopeless." Your body has never felt like it's *allowed* to feel what it feels. Give yourself permission to feel whatever arises. You're learning to trust your body again. And your body is learning to trust you. I believe that a chronic state of an emotion can be caused by repressing feelings that want to be felt. John Bradshaw says, "You can't heal what you can't feel."

As you allow these parts to be and love them anyway, you are holding space for them to feel safe and acknowledged, and that is what these parts are looking for. Like young children not getting a parent's attention, they've been getting louder and louder. Now that they have your attention, just be with them the way the most loving mother would be with her child. By doing so, you expand.

BREATHWORK

One of the most potent tools I've found is equal parts unraveling the nervous system, releasing contraction in the body, and expanding your upper limits for expansion. It is called 3-part circular breathwork. This tool is especially useful for those of us who find sitting still in meditation difficult. It's a full-body experience. You'll notice physical, mental, emotional, and (for some) spiritual sensations. Three-part breathwork can take you to non-ordinary states of consciousness.

This breathwork quiets the mind (specifically your prefrontal cortex), so you can process, release, and integrate what's being held subconsciously in the body. Every session is different. Sometimes you'll get visions and insights. Sometimes you'll process sadness or elation. Sometimes you'll want to yell, write down a strategy, or take immediate action on your inspiration. Whatever comes up is exactly what you need in that session.

Physically, you may feel your body temperature get hot or cold, tingling, or wrist cramping into what we endearingly call "lobster claws" (scientifically called tetany, a result of creating more alkaline blood). Physical sensations disappear as soon as you resume breathing normally in through the nose and out through your mouth. You may get creative downloads or access memories. You may experience spontaneous crying or laughter. You may have an out-of-body experience, feel one with God, converse with your higher self. Whatever arises is perfect.

Energy moves through breath, movement, and sound. This tool focuses on breath and sound. The technique gives your left brain something to do to keep it busy so you can access your right brain: your subconscious, creativity, and intuition—your door to expansion. What does it look like? This breath is all through your mouth, not your nose. Lay down on your back, and put one hand on your stomach and one hand on your chest. Close your eyes. Breathe in through your mouth into your stomach (you can feel your stomach lift with air), then without exhaling, breathe in again into your chest (you can feel your chest rise), and then release out of your mouth (not forcefully, just like a water fountain flowing). That's it. It's circular so no rest at the bottom or top of the breath; it's continuous 3-part breathing. Open mouth, breathe into the stomach, top off with your chest, release, and repeat. Take full, deep breaths and enjoy the ride! I recommend 20 to 30 minutes of this 3-part breathing. It takes about 10 minutes to hit cruising altitude. The first 10 minutes can feel like the first 10 minutes of a run. You may need to motivate yourself. After 10 minutes, the breath breathes you.

This is an active, engaging experience so it's much easier for my clients to do this than to quiet their minds in stillness for meditation. Meditation can take months or even years of dedicated practice, and it can be especially challenging and frustrating if your nervous system is particularly wound up. As you feel and release the energy patterns through breathwork and other tools, you'll gradually reprogram your nervous system, feeling better physically, emotionally and mentally. These changes rewire your subconscious at the deepest levels.

I like to play music without words (so the mind doesn't get caught up in the lyrics) to get into the body. Play around with tempos and genres to see how different music inspires different experiences.

Throughout the 3-part breath, you can tone—make sounds on your exhale. You may start a little shy, with an audible exhale. Then you'll start feeling comfortable releasing screams, moans, even surprising yourself with sounds you've never made or heard. Everything you're feeling and expressing through this breath and sound is releasing, further unraveling your nervous system, so you can free bound up energy patterns. It's coming up to go out.

One thing I appreciate about this tool is it's free. Anyone who can breathe has access to it. To date, nobody has hurt themselves or died from doing this breathwork, so it's safe to do by yourself. Feel free to lay on a yoga mat, cover your eyes, and place a pillow under your knees if you'd like. I recommend not having anything under your head to keep your air passageway open so you can take in maximum breaths. My clients and I love to write things down afterward: visions, creative ideas, business strategies, or bold new actions to take.

If, during the first few times, you only notice some physical sensations, your nervous system is unfurling, relaxing to feel safe, and creating more space to experience mental, emotional, or spiritual sensations. Amazing work! The best way to make the most of your breathwork experience is to go in with an open mind, with no expectations, no attachment to any outcome, fully surrender to the experience, and trust your breath.

Breathwork has become mental and emotional hygiene for me. I practice this a few times a week. Usually it's on the days that I don't feel like doing it that I have the most powerful sessions. Funny how our minds know how to avoid feeling things.

> You can access a recording of my free guided "Alchemy Breathwork" experience on my website at www.victoriasong.me/bending-reality.

This breathwork is effective because it allows you to release what's been stored in your body. It's similar to how a gazelle can be chased all day every day in nature, continuously threatened, and not be traumatized. Once the gazelle is safe and stops running, it shakes its entire body. It releases all that adrenaline and cortisol, the hormones that accompany fear, contraction, and the tightening of the nervous system. It lets all of that move through its system. It's meant to be felt and released in the moment. Then the gazelle relaxes again. Even my dog shakes multiple times a day. While historically, the threat to humans might have been a lion; in the modern world, an unexpected email can trigger the same fight-or-flight response.

It's time to stop thinking the laws of nature don't apply to us. Instead of trying to mentally will yourself to move on, focus on the bright side or override a feeling, just *shake it out*. Move it through breath, movement, or sound. Make sure stress and anxiety do not build up in your nervous system. Otherwise you'll continue building up layers and layers of non-completed energy in your body that create the persona of an inflamed ego.

MEDICINE JOURNEYS

Some people want to taste expansion through a medicine journey. During a medicine journey, the default mode network goes down, creating more space temporarily for the unknown. Your normal filters dissolve. The efficient neural pathways that allow you to go on autopilot 95 percent of the time recede. Whatever is usually suppressed by the brain is available. For a moment you have a lens on reality that feels like a child's. You see the world with fresh eyes, making new connections and experiencing it outside default pathways. The walls of reality feel liquid. Your circuits are open, and your thoughts quickly become your reality.

I see many who awaken to new insights, love, the feeling that we're all one, but these expansive truths cannot fit into their nervous system when the journey is over. Remember your nervous system dictates the bandwidth of reality you can take in. You must continue cultivating expansion by unraveling your nervous system in order to integrate what you've touched in your medicine journey.

If you'd like to experience a guided journey, you can find my audio tracks on my website www.victoriasong.me/journeys for intentions ranging from "I Release Control" to "Remember Your Future."

TRUST YOUR INSTINCTS

Reality is so much bigger than our minds. Scientists still debate exactly what percentage of our brain capacity we have access to. Human consciousness is limited to the experiences of the body, its sensations, and yet most of us are not even connected to the emotions, feelings, and sensations in our bodies. To understand the world more completely, it's time to bring the wisdom of the emotions and the body online.

I wonder if Steve Jobs[29] was aware of the limitations of the mind in his Stanford commencement speech June 2005, *"You can't connect the dots looking forward; you can only connect them looking backward. So you have to trust that they will somehow connect in your future."* Jobs certainly understood the power of creating a reality distortion field. The greater my clients and I expand, the more we realize how much the mind seems to be the last to be informed. If you had asked us in the moment of deciding why we went left instead of right, we'd either say, "I don't know" or looking back we'd rationalize what we chose. These dots are not just major events that happen in weeks, months, and years. We start to connect the dots in moments—three seconds at a time—the seemingly random, micro-actions we take throughout a day.

It's easy for most people to see how some of the important events of our lives, such as major career moves, relationships, and professional outcomes, came about from what seemed at the time an inconsequential decision. My clients and I experience such synchronicity daily, where within minutes and even seconds, we get the feedback loop of "glad I turned left!" They experience meaningful coincidences in

the form of flight delays that lead to key connections, critical information from an unlikely place, significant happy accidents, being at
the right place at the right time, and things happening in no time
at all. Based on my experiences of synchronicity, I now believe that
reality is not linear; however, our minds cannot wrap itself around
a non-linear reality. It's almost like an ant contemplating the vast-
ness of the world; our minds are not equipped to take it all in. So
we work within the constraints of what makes sense to the mind,
even if it's only able to take in 5 percent of reality. The experience of
synchronicity may be our closest experience of time.

I can hold this possibility in a state of expansion, how about
you? Humans seem to believe that, *"If it were true, it would make
sense to us."* What if we understood so much less than we realize? Does that unknown feel a little scary? If things are not what they seem to the mind, does considering that possibility create contraction in your body? If so, don't worry about it. Revisit it when you feel more expanded and see how it feels then. Trust how you feel in every moment. Do not override where you are right now. I do not convince my clients of anything. We simply unwind the nervous system to hold more perspectives so we can access deeper levels of truth.

Most of us believe our mind is the smartest part of us. In this way, the mind has become a great blind spot.

When the mind honestly doesn't know why we turned left instead
of right, it appears random because most of us believe our mind is
the smartest part of us. In this way, the mind has become a great
blind spot.

As you develop your emotional intelligence and your body intelligence, you learn to value your emotions, intuition, and sensations,
and also to trust them. You see that they hold wisdom beyond your
mind that you can empirically test. When synchronicities happen
these days, my clients are delighted and amazed, but no longer
surprised. Surprise happens when an event occurs outside your

expectations. Now they say, "It's a new normal." They welcome the outcome with gratitude.

Do you trust your instincts? What's your relationship to synchronicity? How much do you rely on your intellect versus your intuition?

PERCEPTION BECOMES REALITY

The mind is incredibly powerful because it can make your body believe it's in whatever state the mind thinks it's in. Your body will trust the environment the mind believes it's in more than the actual state of reality and create a physiological response to this regardless of whether it's accurate. This is how we participate in the creation of reality through our witnessing. If we fall into contraction, we find reasons for contraction all around us. If we consciously choose to move into expansion, we can create a different reality.

Notice what you allow to influence your perception. Watch who and what you let shape it: advertisements, news, friends, family, politicians, movies, entertainment, TV programing, media. Collective perception creates society. If the media paint the picture of a dangerous, divisive "Us vs. Them" world, we will fear one another and live in a world of fear. The more humans live in their heads, contracted and disconnected from their supernatural abilities, the more easily programmable they are. Writer Alice Walker said, "The most common way people give up their power is by thinking they don't have any." Sprinkle in some fear (so we become desperate to survive) and shame (so we judge one another and ourselves, creating more separation) to a population in contraction and you've got people in panic, desperate for any solution to rescue them. They'll feel like a Victim, blame a Villain, and name a Hero to save the day.

Are you done letting anyone tell you what to think, do, be, and say? To go off the well-worn, paved path requires a willingness to sit in uncertainty. As we have learned, the more contracted and wound up the nervous system is, the less able you are to sit with uncertainty. It's too uncomfortable. Grabbing for safety and a false sense of certainty is what keeps most marching to the beat of station 94.7.

Notice what keeps you from speaking your truth, sharing your feelings or standing out. What part of you is afraid of being different? Which part is scared of being laughed at, judged, or shamed? Where are you not speaking your truth and going along with someone else's reality?

There is a different channel that is attuned to amplify you. On this channel, you will receive more than you can imagine. To tune into your channel, release your contractions and follow your expansion. We each have something within us that only we can bring to life. We connect to it when we are in expansion. Who you are naturally, your essence, your unique expression is your most expanded self. This is your greatest contribution to humanity.

EXERCISE: TOOLS FOR RELEASING CONTRACTION

Here are some more tools, in no particular order, that have been effective for me and my clients in releasing contraction. Choose one or two (or more) to try this week.

1. Scream into a pillow, or underwater to protect your vocal cords, while you let it rip: put chin down and out to open the throat.
2. Whip the floor with a towel. (Bonus: use a wet towel for even more impact.)
3. Talk back to your inner critic. Do not let it speak freely without any push-back.
4. Move energy through breath, movement, or sound with yoga, dance, meditation, toning, singing, screaming, breathwork, and moving your body.
5. Neutralize a charge. For every con/negative, think of a pro/positive to offset and balance it to neutral. Write down equal pros and cons to every outcome, event, or decision.
6. Turn up music that goes with the emotion you're feeling. Stomp your rage, crawl your grief, or dance it out.
7. Practice screaming, making any sounds in the privacy of your car with the bonus of traffic as a trigger.
8. Share with someone you're comfortable crying in front of and let your tears do the talking, moaning, and yelping. Make all the sounds with *few to no words*.
9. Pretend you're any animal—lion, bird, dog, for example—and make the sound that reflects how you feel.
10. Take the shape of your emotion. Curl up into a ball, get small, kneel down, or get big, stomp around the floor or jump up and down, move the way this emotion would, dramatize it like you were acting in drama club.
11. Get a deep tissue massage, remove the areas of tension

in your body, but not so much pressure that the muscles contract in response, just the right amount of pressure that the body can surrender to. Use breath and sound to release what's stuck.

12. Stretch. Notice where the body is tight and bring blood circulation there. Release any sound or breath that goes with the stretching.

13. Share your pain, struggle, fear, hurt, sadness whatever is holding contraction and let it be witnessed. Speaking its truth releases it. You can say, "A part of me feels . . . " and feel it without letting it define you.

14. Write down what you're feeling: your judgments, your fears, your rawest version of truth that no one will see but you.

15. Write an unfiltered letter (that you don't send) saying everything you've been holding in that you'd say if the other person could really hear you.

16. Make a list of your parents' characteristics ("positive" and "negative") and their worldviews. Then write how those qualities and worldviews show up in you and decide what you want to release.

17. Make a list of the traits of your parents' relationship together, how those relationship characteristics show up in your relationships, and decide what you want to release.

18. Show yourself empathy. Release shame, guilt, self-hate, self-judgment. When you catch yourself being hard on yourself or creating any contraction through self-directed thoughts, stop and say, "Thank you, I love you. You're safe" to yourself. Feel your body soften.

19. Reflect on the greatest hardships, lowest lows, even traumas in your history and find the gift in it. Feel how it shaped what you care about, your strength, your resilience, who you became and all the positive ripples it had on your life. Feel what owning your story feels like in your body.

CHAPTER 7
The Secret Behind Self-Development Tools

WHY DO SO MANY SELF-DEVELOPMENT TOOLS SEEM TO work? Because there are many ways to access expansion. For some, the more mysterious occult is interesting. For others, the simpler, the better. For some, it needs to feel like an esoteric secret or else everyone would've figured it out. For others, they want simple, accessible universal language.

I notice people study vertically, a modality for 10-plus years, or a lifetime with a guru, believing this guru has *the* answer. The approaches vary widely: meditation, yoga, therapy, family constellations, peak performance, NPL, SRI, EFT, IFS, shamans, tantra, reiki, chakras, somatic, plant medicine, chi gong, acupuncture, inner child work, and breathwork are just some examples. The Masters appear supernatural because they have freed up their nervous systems and mastered expansion in their bodies. As a result, they have the heart of a child (open and available to feel everything) and the mind of a sage. They've opened up their circuits to receive infinite intelligence and they may truly believe their path is the only one that can lead others to similar supernatural abilities.

Supernatural abilities are available at all times; however, in contraction, you block off your access. In spiritual communities, people refer to those who have access to these abilities as "tapped in." Once you're aware of how to release contraction so you can be in expansion, you'll be tapped in all the time. People refer to those who are tapped in all the time as Masters. But *you* can do that. It's the mastery of expansion. The Masters with whom I've trained had access to what appeared to my consciousness at the time as supernatural abilities. These abilities have come alive for me and my clients ever since we did the work I laid out in this book.

THE SIMPLICITY BEHIND THE COMPLEXITY

I've been studying horizontally. Every self-development tool, coach, and book I've experienced is a vehicle to help you move through contraction and into expansion. Some teachers may not even realize this common denominator as they may be very attached to their proprietary tool or method, but they are all different ways of getting to the same thing. As I stated, it's *simple* but *not easy* because it goes against everything we've learned.

For instance, Co-Active,[30] the world's largest in-person coach training school, teaches three main modules: 1. Fulfillment, 2. Balance 3. Process. In Fulfillment, you're trained how to effectively determine your client's values, sense of life purpose, and connection to their higher self. You learn how to attune to what lights them up, what makes them feel most alive, what truly matters to them. This work gets your client into expansion. In this module, you're also trained to listen for the voice of the "Saboteur," which is the client's inner critic voice(s). Or what I call the voice of contraction. This voice gets in the way of expansion with messages such as, "I can't," "I have to," "I shouldn't," and "It's just the way it is." It comprises the limiting beliefs, stories, and assumptions from which the client is operating, but isn't aware are not true. It's what keeps the client working "inside the box" vs. able to look "outside the box." The Saboteur holds all the thoughts, beliefs, and programming that keep the client from creating what they truly want. It blocks them from what will bring them joy, fulfillment, and aliveness. You're basically looking for all the places your client is holding contraction so you can guide them to operate from expansion through their vision, values, life purpose, and higher self.

In the Process module, you're trained on how to help your client process their emotions. You learn how to effectively bring your client down into the emotion so they can experience it completely, noticing the sensations, imagery, and emotions that arise. You learn the skill of helping them allow, accept, and embrace their feelings so they can complete and release the stuck energy patterns and access new awareness and perspectives. You support your client in fully feeling what's underneath the contraction, so it can be released.

> **I have categorized *every* tool, exercise, concept I've ever learned and lived into two categories: remove contraction and increase expansion.**

In the balance module, you're trained on how to help your client find an elevated perspective beyond the one they're currently stuck in. As mentioned, when someone is in contraction, they tend to see black-and-white options: choice A or choice B. They see problems. When someone is in expansion, they transcend "either/or" thinking and have access to new opportunities and solutions.

While these curriculums and trainings don't speak in terms of expansion and contraction, this is the common denominator behind everything I've seen. I have categorized *every* tool, exercise, and concept I've ever learned and lived into two categories: remove contraction and increase expansion. My toolkit is a large assortment of ways to identify and remove contraction, and support clients into greater expansion.

I've seen some programs and tools that are focused only on expansion such as start a gratitude practice, create your vision, connect to your higher self, visualize what you want, meditate, determine your values, discover your life purpose, do what you love, enjoy the present moment. Many coaching events and programs will empower its participants to feel confident, capable, and motivated. During the experience, you reach peak expansion and feel brand new with limitless possibilities. And then when the experience ends, contraction sets back in because you didn't release your contractions. If you want long-lasting change, you need to feel and release your contractions. Otherwise, you can become addicted to expansion events, and always look for the next workshop, program, or peak experience to get you back into expansion. I've also seen programs and tools focus on removing contraction such as excavate limiting beliefs, tapping, reiki, feeling emotions, neutralize charges, trauma release, inner critic dialogue, and forgiveness work.

> **Here is your eighth unlearning:** *If you only focus on expansion, you are bypassing what needs to be seen and capping your upper limits on expansion. If you're just focused on removing contraction, you miss what's possible when you entrain your nervous system to expansion. Combining the two is where the magic happens.*

Why is there a coach for just about every topic under the sun?

Life coaching, career coaching, leadership coaching, team coaching, relationship coaching, dating coaching, female empowerment coaching, men's coaching, money coaching, sex coaching, health coaching, spiritual coaching, family coaching. Because for every topic, you'll find the programming, patterns, beliefs, and insecurities that hold contraction and keep you from expansion in that area of your life. The coach on that topic has usually mastered contraction in that area of their life and has a set of tools, frameworks, steps, and methods to help you master that area as well. So while everyone is programmed to live and operate mostly from contraction, everyone has a different access point to doing this work based on where they feel the most pain and therefore, the most motivation to do something about the pain. Some are motivated by a desire to grow—to reach their fullest potential. Many of my clients are highly motivated to be the best leaders they can be so that they can build the most successful companies possible. For others, they may be burned out working jobs that don't matter to them and are ready to find work that's aligned with their passion, so they hire a career coach. Others may be struggling in their romantic relationships but feel stuck repeating old patterns, so they hire a relationship coach.

Your access point will likely be the area of your life where the contraction is painful enough that you're willing to get support for it. You're willing to invest the time, money, and energy into removing this contraction. You may be part of a small and growing number of people who value growth in key areas of their life and want to reach their full potential.

EXPANSION FROM TRAUMA

I believe some of the greatest Masters have been through some of the most severe traumas I've heard of. Trauma results from overwhelming the nervous system to the extent that it exceeds a person's ability to cope or integrate the emotions involved in that experience. This is especially common if the trauma occurs during childhood. It can be particularly difficult for these individuals to feel emotions because opening up to feel them lets in a lot of pain. But if they don't feel it, the pain doesn't go anywhere. Many will find ways to self-medicate that pain, others will unconsciously repeat the cycles causing pain to others, and some will choose to face their pain, to go on a long journey of unwinding their nervous system, removing contraction, and finding their path to expansion.

It's too difficult for those who've been abused or experienced severe trauma to even attempt to live according to the normal 94.7. When someone has gone through severe trauma, their nervous system is particularly wound up. The body does not feel safe. They often live even more in their head and disconnected from their body. As a child, they often lived in their imagination, creating worlds in their mind where they felt safe.

In my work, I've found that some of the most successful, visionary people have had some of the greatest wounds, have endured tremendous contraction, and are on their path to finding access to expansion. They also have a high tolerance for contraction because in many ways their life today is easy-breezy compared to what they've been through, so they have a higher set point for what triggers them into contraction. They already have a relationship with discomfort and pain. They know they can live through it. They know they can do hard. For many of them, the worst moments of their lives are behind them. I believe those with the greatest wounds have access to the greatest gifts. However, until the contraction is felt and transmuted into expansion, they're living from the wound of their history versus living from the gift of their history.

This is why I sought out 24 coaches, therapists, and spiritual masters. I was completely out of my body, numb to it. My body did not feel safe and I was disconnected from my emotions. I didn't know how to be with all the emotions I had bottled up over the years: pain, fear, grief, anger, suffering that went unexpressed because I told no one what was happening. I told no one how as a little girl, from the ages of 7 to 17 years old, bruised and bleeding, scared for my life, I cried on my knees and screamed at God, asking, "Why? I never asked to be born!"

Growing up, I escaped the chaos through school. I doubled down on my mind, got into Yale University, Harvard Business School, startup investing at 23 years old, and was on the Forbes 30 Under 30 list for my industry. And I was *empty* inside. The most painful contraction showed up in my romantic relationships. I dated narcissists, sociopaths, rapists, and physically and emotionally abusive men.

This pattern continued until I stopped looking to fix myself and instead started *feeling* myself. I went on my own journey to unravel my nervous system, identify and release contraction, and access greater expansion. I brought the same rigor to my journey that

I'd brought to my academic studies and discovered what has been hiding in plain sight, available to all of us.

To evolve to our fullest potential, we must be accountable for our internal state of contraction or expansion. It's the mark of "growing up" and becoming an adult. Until we see the role we play in all of it, we cannot change any of it. Do we blame others, or do we fully own from where we make our choices? We may not be responsible for our history, but we are responsible for healing any trauma so we can release our contractions. The consequences of choices made from expansion look very different from those made from contraction. Which way do you want to bend reality?

You can't fake where you are. An emotion only feels like suffering as long as you refuse to experience it. It can even be painful to mentally tell yourself how you *should* feel and try to will your emotions and body to follow. Welcome every sensation and emotion without needing to analyze the experience. Just by feeling it fully, you loosen the nervous system memory and it dissipates. Keep releasing all the areas of contraction by moving the stuck energy patterns through the tools in this book and any other tools you find that support you in unraveling your nervous system.

FAITH, TRUST, AND EXPANSION

Faith and trust create expansion in your system, so faith and trust in whatever you're trying is what allows whatever you do to work. This is a fascinating capability of our consciousness.

What should you believe makes this possible?

Whatever would be fun, inspiring, and expansive to believe. Some clients believe in the magic of synchronicity. One client believes his mother is looking over him. Some believe it's a game with Easter eggs or a scavenger hunt. Some believe it's a simulation. If believing in God makes you feel expansive, do that! If believing in aliens makes you feel expansive, do that! If you notice yourself feel contracted, judging, and not wanting to look stupid believing in something, then explore that contraction.

What works?

Whatever gets you into expansion. Expansion is what works. It has power over our physical world. I believe this is why prayer appears to work for those who swear by it. When you pray, you trust that a god is listening and able to give you what you're praying for. You're grateful in advance with faith that it's already done. It's like being open and expanded, envisioning what you want, and manifesting it. It's focusing without any effort or tension but with deep relaxation.

Religious faith or a structured belief system is not the only means of accessing this kind of expansion. Some clients find solutions while they're in the shower, when their nervous systems are relaxed and expanded (not trying hard to solve a problem, which puts them into contraction). Others say their best thinking happens when they're running (releasing energy patterns through movement—open and expanded) or first thing in the morning when they're a blank slate for the day, an open vessel that hasn't been filled with all the day's contractive thoughts. Some feel this after a glass of wine, while they're taking a walk outside, or even while they're sleeping and wake up with a solution. Heck, it's why aromatherapy works. When you smell something beautiful, you're in expansion and your nervous system relaxes. I imagine it's why lucky charms "work." Wall Street traders believe in their lucky socks. Bowlers carry their lucky ball, or a baseball player eats fried chicken before every game. It's their belief, trust, faith (relaxed nervous system, expansion) that give the charm power.

Expansion is what works.

Henry Ford said, "Whether you think you can or you can't, you're right."[31] I believe expansion is the reason for the placebo effect.[32] If a person expects a pill to do something, then it's possible that the body's own chemistry can create effects similar to what a medication might have caused. *Perception becomes reality.* This is why double-blind placebo studies are considered the gold standard where the experimenters and participants are "blind" to who gets the placebo. Drugs must outperform the placebo in order to have any viability. In one depression study, only 25 percent of recovered participants was attributed to the actual chemicals of the antidepressant.[33] For the rest, I believe being in a state of expansion throughout the study period, believing and trusting they'll get better, is what healed them. Once they'd embodied the new possibility of being healthy, whole, and healed, they bent their reality. Instead of feeling the contraction of the current circumstance (depression), they began to hold the feeling of expansion of a new possibility, which became their new reality. Where in your life are you holding the circumstances (contraction) instead of the vision of what you want to happen (expansion)?

The key to mastering the outer world is mastery over your inner world. Now that you know, you'll see expansion everywhere. Imagine what would be possible if you were able to cultivate expansion, so you could operate from and live from expansion all day, every day?

I've seen (expansion) Masters heal diseases in people who were given months to live, intuitively know what's going on in the body without any medical information, channel information from loved ones who've passed over, and share words that were private to that relationship. I've witnessed Masters send and receive information telepathically, read information densities invisible to the naked eye, travel in dreams to other's dreams, and receive detailed clairvoyant premonitions. They've come back after near-death experiences, accessed super-senses (beyond audio, sight, touch, taste, scent), instantaneously manifested visions into reality, abilities that appear supernatural to your current state of consciousness.

THE POWER OF UNQUESTIONABLE BELIEF

In our society, we laugh at gullible people, thinking they're dumb, naïve, and unlikely to survive natural selection. Skepticism seems synonymous with intelligence. I believe this explains the waves we're seeing in the self-development world, the rate at which we're reaching the tipping point of people looking for another way to live life to its fullest. You could say the "gullible ones" who are easily persuaded to believe anything that sounds promising took to the book *The Secret*[34] in 2006, which sold 30 million copies worldwide and has been translated into 50 languages. The book is based on the belief in the law of attraction—a philosophy that suggests positive thoughts bring positive results and negative thoughts bring negative outcomes. Some well-known successes such as Oprah championed it saying the book's message is one she's been sharing with the world on her show for the past couple decades. While many swear by *The Secret,* the rest of the world rejected it saying there is no scientific foundation, merely clichéd "truisms and magical thinking presented as hidden knowledge."[35]

For most of the world, *The Secret* set off the bullshit detector. Your bullshit detector is your nervous system speaking up. Try saying this to yourself, "I am powerful, wise, and abundant"[36] and see how that lands in your body. If you feel resonance and find yourself *feeling,* "YES!", that is all you have to say to remind yourself to get into expansion.

If you experience any resistance, judgment, discomfort, or find it hard to believe—good noticing! This is a sign you get to explore where there's contraction blocking you from living in expansion. Whatever is in the way is what you get to release by feeling. If you're numb or feel nothing, this is good awareness. Your nervous system is likely doing this to protect itself from feeling too much of anything.

The key here is how it lands in the body. If there's any doubt, resistance, or numbness, then the belief is not resonant. You're looking for what clears your system. Your system is the bullshit detector.

For example, try feeling into this belief: "I can fly." Most likely your mind immediately thinks, "No, I can't." Then your body laughs and rejects this statement. You may tense up. Notice that the statement bounces out.

Now try feeling into this belief: "I can do this." Notice how it lands and expands in your body. Feel the resonance.

This is the difference to look for.

As long as the beliefs are held resonant in the body, clearing your system's bullshit detector, then they *can* work. This brings us to the next wave, of which I believe Dr. Joe Dispenza's work[37] is an example.

He researches the fields of neuroscience, epigenetics, and quantum physics to explore the science behind how people can heal themselves of illnesses, chronic conditions, and even terminal diseases. For those who are open-minded and on the fence about *The Secret*, his work has "enough science" to make them believers. Many who attend his events claim healing miracles.

In some ways, those who can be selectively gullible—unquestionably believe—are the lucky ones if they can use it intentionally because *you cannot have what you don't believe you can have*. However, there's a fine line between expansion and resisting contraction. Resisting contraction is the equivalent of being an optimist who's in denial. In the spiritual community, this is called spiritual bypassing, a term introduced by John Welwood, a Buddhist teacher and psychotherapist. Welwood defines it as "the tendency to use spiritual ideas and practices to sidestep or avoid facing unresolved emotional issues, psychological wounds, and unfinished developmental tasks."[38] Since facing our contractions can be uncomfortable, many would rather say, "I'm broke, but I'm going to manifest money. I trust God will provide."

I believe the next wave required to reach a tipping point is removing contraction to create space in the nervous system for new beliefs to land and expand without requiring any preconditions, beliefs, or leaps of faith. I don't use faith or science to convince, but rather I encourage you to use your personal experience to gain supernatural access.

A WORD OF CAUTION

You may catch yourself becoming a superstitious lab rat and try every self-development offering under the sun like I did. Remember the ones in Skinner's experiment?[39] The rats were given food with no reference to the rat's behavior. Then the rat associated the delivery of food with whatever chance action they had been performing as it was delivered and continued to perform these same actions.

When spiritual leaders do not feel, release, and integrate their parts that hold contraction (and instead chase expansion), it can lead to dysfunction. I've seen some weird rituals, cults and false gods in the communities of such leaders. If you find yourself in a sequence that doesn't feel good or goes against your moral compass, question the why and see if the leader may be misguided and convinced this works because of their unique *how*. Their followers feel amazing because expansion = supernatural access, especially when a group comes together and uses their collective, expansive consciousness to bend reality. See if the framework here of removing contraction and increasing expansion can explain the results so you can steer clear of anyone who thinks, *I'm chosen with so much power, follow me.*

From what I've seen, it appears that many coaches and teachers know what (and even how) it works, but they don't know *why it works*, so you may also be getting their superstitious assembly of steps, tools, and methodology. While the mind wants to complicate it, it is simple.

Do not resist feeling the contraction. You must release contraction in order to access and stabilize expansion. There are many who seek the light, want to be the light, and stay in the light. But you can only shine as bright as you are willing to travel to the darkest aspects of your contractions. Your densest contractions conceal your highest expansion. Embrace them. The elixir is always found in the underworld.

Let how you feel become your beacon. Notice what you notice. Do not override what you feel. The more often you pay attention, the faster you'll begin to rewire your nervous system to expansion. The most enlightened humans I know are attuned to their nervous system. Release any expectations of what feeling your emotions will be like including judgment of "I've already felt this." Crying, hurting, anger, fear, and feeling emotions are not signs that something is wrong, needs fixing, or that you're still not healed. Quite the contrary. *They're signs of progress* that you've unraveled your nervous system to have more emotions be available to you.

« »

The journey into expansion requires mastery over mind, body, and emotions. You access the zero-point field/quantum field/field of infinite possibilities and probabilities when you've entered deep expansion where you dissolve into oneness, a feeling of nothingness and everythingness at the same time. As your sense of separateness dissolves, your supernatural abilities of psychic perception and downloads, synchronicities, and manifested visions—all capabilities of your consciousness—increase. Again, these abilities only appear supernatural when you don't realize all that your consciousness is capable of. As your consciousness expands, you see reality more clearly. Shifts in perception are a natural byproduct of a widening consciousness. To further expand your consciousness, feel and release your emotions every time you notice them. By letting all energy patterns flow through you, you clear your system of anything blocking your access to the expansive state required to bend reality.

Remember, we don't see reality as it is. We see it through our level of consciousness, so our work is about expanding our consciousness to upgrade our lens on reality. When you expand, everything around you elevates beyond what you could have hoped for or imagined. The most common response I get when my clients experience this is, "My life improved in ways I *couldn't imagine*." Have you done the work to create from expansion where you access creative downloads, visions, genius, infinite intelligence, your unique supernatural abilities, the edges of the hologram or simulation?

All the coaches and programs I've seen believe what they're teaching works, because it can work. *But it's not the only thing that works.* They're all different ways of getting to the same thing. The Masters appear to have supernatural abilities because they've cultivated and mastered expansion.

If ice cream got you into expansion, I'd say, "Think about ice cream." Think less about the word or symbol and more about the *feeling of expansion* in the body. What's the feeling behind gratitude, faith, trust, love, joy, truth, purpose, pleasure, freedom, fun, or surrender?

EXERCISE: HOW WELL CAN YOU IDENTIFY THE SPECTRUM FROM CONTRACTION TO EXPANSION?

Now let's see how well you've mastered understanding contraction and expansion by assessing each of the following on a scale where 1 is ultimate contraction and 10 is ultimate expansion.

I feel shame, I'm a fraud _____.

I feel anxious and scared _____.

I want it so badly _____.

I feel like no matter what, I'll be okay _____.

I feel optimistic _____.

I feel calm _____.

I feel present as pure awareness _____.

As you feel into each of these statements, you can also feel the varying degrees of contraction and expansion in the body. Shame feels like a deeper contraction than fear. Trusting you'll be okay no matter what feels expansive. Feeling optimistic feels even more expansive. Feeling inner peace feels even more expansive. Feeling present as pure awareness feels the most expansive. Don't take my word for it; feel into it yourself and see how contracted or expanded you feel in each of these statements.

CHAPTER 8
Are You an Expert or a Master?

NOT ONLY DOES EXPANSION CREATE EPIC RESULTS, you can also trust what you create from here. You feel abundant, trusting, open, and more aware of your interconnectedness with everything around you, so your solutions will be win-win-win. In contraction, you may sense scarcity, be scared of the unknown in survival mode, and believe your narrow bandwidth on reality is all that exists. You may believe that life is your circumstances, and you can't see what else is possible. You may hold onto your opinion or judgment as fact, filtering for what justifies it. From this place, you'll create zero-sum solutions: how to get more and more of the scarce resources for you, your family, and your company. You'll be focused on the bottom line without concern for any non-financial impact on people or the planet.

From contraction, you'll go to war for these limited resources because fight-flight is the solution set you have access to here. You'll concentrate on protecting yourself because you perceive a dog-eat-dog world out there. You'll feel separate and isolate yourself, feeling more and more alone. You'll prioritize cutting costs instead of investing in innovation. You'll compete instead of collaborate. You'll be motivated by power over others, control, and owning more. You'll fixate on killing diseases instead of boosting your immune system to prevent diseases. You'll be focused on job security, the white picket fence, a few vacations, and a good retirement. As Kyle Cease describes it, "You'll put a bunch of locks on a door to a life you're not fully living in order to feel safe, not realizing that the more you fully live, the less afraid you are of dying."[40] In contraction, you're burned out and exhausted. There isn't enough time, money, or energy. By operating from here, we've created a world that is in contraction. The system is based in contraction and its engine is designed to perpetuate contraction through what it values.

In expansion, you connect to acceptance, empathy, creativity, solutions, flow state—the field of infinite possibilities and probabilities. From here, you sense abundance. Your nervous system is relaxed and your bandwidth on reality is expanded. You can be with the unknown. You're energized because you've freed up all that energy that was bound up in contraction. Expansion is your renewable, sustainable energy. You no longer see black-and-white in judgment or polarity but can hold multiple perspectives in neutrality. You see clearly.

By releasing contraction to enter expansion, you access new insights, a new perception of reality that you've never seen before. From this place, you create win-win-win solutions: how to grow the pie, how to innovate for the best and highest of all. You feel safe and taken care of, so you focus on how to serve others. You realize how inefficient selfishness is in such an interconnected world. You find fun, meaningful ways to grow and contribute to a positive future for the world. You are inspired by diversity instead of threatened by it. You spend your energy on people, places, and things that you love and that excite you. You have a passion for life that is infectious. You courageously make your dreams a reality and you are eternally grateful for and celebrate all the good in life. You gain wisdom from every experience and you effortlessly emanate love and compassion for others. You enjoy experiences that expand your consciousness and desire to take as many people as you can with you. In expansion, you may see death as your consciousness expanding beyond your body.

In contraction, this game called Life feels like a single-player game where the way to win is to uplevel with more money, more success, and more status. In expansion, you see that there's a secret way to win that comes from realizing we're all in this together. Your contractions are humanity's contractions. It is what connects us all together. What you cannot transmute in you, you project out there. The suffering in the world is a projection of the untransmuted contraction that exists in each of us and in all of us. When you're able to see and own your unconscious projections, you bring light to the collective shadow. Face and release your unconscious fears. When you

While contraction can create experts, expansion creates masters.

do, you release them from the collective contraction. None of us make it out of this game alive. This realization naturally leads us into service. While in contraction, suffering pushes people apart. In expansion, suffering brings people together.

From expansion, you create from nothing in no time. You're freed from old reference points, including who you thought you were. As your identity is released, you become an empty vessel for life, downloads, and your supernatural abilities. While contraction can create experts, expansion creates Masters. When you sit in the spaciousness of expansion as pure awareness of whatever arises, you access magic.

In my 20s, my personal definition of "success" was surprising myself with things I didn't know I could do, jumping at opportunities to build my courage, self-trust, and confidence. I celebrated the version of me I saw and became on the other side. In expansion, it's not even about success or failure anymore. You transcend the polarity thinking of contraction. The process of creation is where the joy lies. Who you become in the process of making your vision happen is what lights you up. The outcomes are just feedback for growth toward further alignment. Since seeing success and failure this way, I've achieved what to the outside world may appear to be improbable "success." If you think you've been able to accomplish a lot in contraction, see how much more you're capable of in expansion.

CREATE YOUR OWN PLAYBOOK

Countless books are sold on the successful habits of others. Once you learn what Steve Jobs did and what Jeff Bezos does, you seek to replicate and become more like them. Most do not realize what you now understand after reading this book: *the moment you try to be anyone but you, you're in contraction and on the path of working harder, longer hours.* If someone you look up to resonates with who you are and amplifies your authenticity, then be inspired! But choosing to follow

The moment you try to be anyone but you, you're in contraction and on the path of working harder, longer hours.

in someone's footsteps because you believe that you'll be successful if you do is going to lead you to a local maximum. Local maxima are the tallest mountains you can see from where you are standing, but not necessarily the tallest mountain of them all: global maximum.

In other words, you may do relatively better than before, but you won't reach your full potential. All the brilliant visionaries march to the beat of their *own* drum. *That's* the part to learn from, not following their unique march. If you are curious about the path of a successful person, instead of following what they do, understand *why* they do it. Then see if you also find their why important to you. For instance, if someone drinks green juice every day, and you discover it's because they believe it makes them healthy, if you value health, find ways to improve your health. You'll probably find better solutions unique to your health than also drinking green juice every day.

Pattern recognition optimizes for local maxima. My goal is not to help a client just improve a business. My aim is to help them—and you—learn how to reach a global maximum—full potential—for your business and create your *own playbook,* not follow someone else's playbook. I want you to learn how to live, lead, and operate from expansion. You'll become able to sit in the uncertainty of the unknown long enough to see reality more clearly than those who grab as quickly as they can for certainty.[41] In the not knowing, new information comes. Relaxing into the unknown with your nervous system open invites intelligent downloads. Your body then recalibrates around this expanded state. From here, you access the field of infinite possibilities and probabilities, and your own supernatural abilities. As my client George Ruan, co-founder and CEO of Honey, once said, "Victoria has a unique ability you cannot learn or teach someone. She helps me figure out how to solve my own problems."

Pattern recognition only takes you so far. Your mind wants to control and predict, so it feels safer following a preexisting playbook. But you also now understand the limitations of seeking safety in the face of the unknown. Any illusion of safety from following another's model that assumes "this is like that other time when XYZ happened to my business" not only may not work, but at best can only lead you to local maxima. My clients do not want to be limited by what they or anyone else has seen or done. They hire world-class leadership teams that have superpowers in their skill gaps but, most importantly, know how to question *why* something is happening and get to the root cause analysis versus assume solutions.

PLEASURE FIRST

We live in a society with maxims such as "No pain, no gain," "You deserve a vacation. You *earned* it," and "I can rest when I'm in the grave!" A friend once said to me, "Health, wealth, and freedom—you only get two of the three at a time." You can enjoy yourself after you retire, when you may have some wealth and freedom, but how about health? How many elderly people would give anything for their health and youth again? When you have your health, you have a million dreams. When you don't have your health, you have *one* dream.

The idea of feeling good seems hedonistic and unproductive. Beating yourself up, pushing yourself to do better, work harder, work smarter, and work faster seems productive and respectable. My clients get epic results because they know how to be in expansion while setting big plans and visions for the future. They've learned how to enjoy themselves in the process of making the impossible probable.

You want everything you want because you think you'll feel expansive when you get there. But if you don't feel expansive on your way there, you won't get there. Or worse, you'll feel empty and burned out when you arrive.

4ᵗʰ CODE TO BENDING REALITY
Be in expansion while you reach for more.

Follow your bliss, pleasure, play, and purpose.

There was a time when I spent thousands of hours in coaching and therapy, looking for what I've come to know as expansion. I intellectually understood my limiting beliefs, trauma, insecurities, and all the places I held contraction. I mentally knew why I moved through life the way I did. I saw my patterns and could predict my triggers. I was an A+ student on mentally understanding all of it. But no matter how self-aware I was, it seemed difficult to translate it into real changes in my life. What was holding me back from the results I wanted when it was crystal clear exactly what I needed to do differently to get them?

You may believe you've already heard, learned, or know something but if your life doesn't show it, *you don't know it.*

A proverb from the Asaro Tribe says, "Knowledge is only rumor until it lives in the body."[42] You may believe you've already heard, learned, or know something but if your life doesn't show it, *you don't know it.*

I was still living in my head, and all my understanding was in my mind. I had not removed the contraction in my physical being at the sensation level. I had talked through my pain and suffering, even cried some, but it was all at the mental level of my story—the thoughts I had about why I feel the way I do. I hadn't yet realized how familiar every newly activated trigger felt in my system. I thought it was about the current situation at work or in my relationship, but as I got out of my head and experienced these energy patterns in my body, I noticed these feelings were quite old. I deeply knew them. They felt like they'd been with me for a long time. These patterns were trapped in my body and ready for me to release them. And until I felt them, I couldn't even access pleasure. There was too much unprocessed contraction in the way of feeling any vibrant energy. It was as if my body was staying numb and desensitized to protect itself from feeling any unpleasant emotion. However, since you cannot selectively experience some emotions and not others, to feel pleasure, I needed to feel all my emotions.

Many teachers and programs focus on the mental part of uncovering your limiting beliefs and stories. You can talk all day for years about your contractions. But until you move into the physical body and release them, you will not be able to embody what you mentally understand. I became fascinated by this gap between how much the mind understands and how little is embodied—the rumor in the mind vs. knowledge in the body. All my personal work and training since has been focused on removing contraction and increasing expansion at the physical level so I can teach you how to embody everything you intellectually understand.

UNCOVER YOUR ORIGINAL NATURE

Our seeking is often driven by a desire to feel good, to feel safe and trust everything will work out. You do, be, and have because you believe it'll make you feel expansive. Our ego and personal agenda think we need to be seen a certain way, amass a certain amount of power, wealth, beauty or success, to feel good. We look out there for the validation we haven't learned how to give ourselves. Expansion is an inside job.

Whether you come from contraction or expansion dictates the quality of your creations and the trajectory of your life. If you've been living in contraction, not only have you not seen reality clearly, you also have *no* idea who you are. You are not the beliefs, stories, conditioning, programming, or wiring you've accumulated. As Michelangelo said, "I simply carved away everything that was not David." It's time to carve away what is not you by letting go of contraction.

We look out there for the validation we haven't learned how to give ourselves.

What is *not you* contracts you. Shed what is *not you*. Your original nature hides behind your contractions. All your attempts to fit in at the expense of your own authenticity will put you into contraction. I believe that suffering, anxiety, and depression come from disconnection to oneself. This disconnection makes us feel contracted and unsafe, which causes us to turn to addictions to self-soothe. Releasing contraction is a process of reconnecting to yourself, feeling safe to be in your own skin, safe to be you.

Imagine you're at the center of an onion, and all your conditioning, programming, and beliefs form the layers of the onion. Each time you fully feel your contraction, you peel back layers of the onion to access deeper layers of truth, getting closer to who you truly are. How much truth you're willing to see, no matter how inconvenient or uncomfortable, dictates how close to the center of the onion you reach. Do not be afraid of your contractions. They are your path to expansion.

EXERCISE: FOLLOW YOUR BLISS

What are your natural skills and talents? What comes effortlessly to you? What is something that brings you pleasure? Schedule a pleasurable activity for this week. If you're ready to really raise your upper limits, put pleasure first at the start of every day this week.

CHAPTER 9
Create Your Path as You Walk It

AS YOU CAN NOW SEE, YOU CANNOT ISOLATE CONTRAC-
tion to any single area of your life. Being in contraction because of
stress from work is going to affect how you show up everywhere
else because you'll be coming from contraction into your romantic
relationship, friendships, family, and health. You can try to put your
best foot forward (feign expansion) for those important moments,
but the truth of how you feel will be felt by those closest to you
because you can't sustain any faked expansion. Your access to supernatural abilities will be blocked by any area holding contraction.

It's best that you start with the contractions of which you're
already aware so you can increase your upper limits on expansion. Notice the triggers of contraction, where you feel activated,
and let it move through you. With every release of contraction, the
new expansion ripples out benefiting all areas of your life. As you
bring up the floor on your lowest contractions, you raise your upper
limits, and your bandwidth on reality expands. Just as you cannot

compartmentalize contraction, you cannot isolate expansion to any single area of your life.

Expansion is not a linear block-and-tackle of specific problems in different areas of your life the way the mind would have it. You cannot anticipate all the ways your new expanded way of being will upgrade every part of your life. You'll make healthier choices and sleep better. You'll experience mind–heart coherence and clarity instead of static and noise. You'll feel inspired, energized, unstoppable. You'll create effortlessly from this place instead of through burnout and fatigue. The more expanded you become, the less energy and willpower are required, as if the universe is conspiring in your favor. You'll draw in different kinds of people who value the real you and repel anyone who doesn't vibe with your expanded self. You will no longer struggle to *make* things happen; you'll only need to *allow* things to happen. There'll be a flow to your days. Time will become an ally as you experience synchronicity. You'll trust things to unfold organically, leading to outcomes beyond your wildest imagination. You'll enjoy your life more, attract fulfilling opportunities, and make more money than you expected. There's no limit to the number of ways your life will uplevel when you expand.

The next time you appreciate someone's mastery, whether it's a violinist, Olympian, or race car driver, notice how effortless it looks. Observe how they've mastered being in expansion even when the pressure is on. Pressure that would put most into contraction. You may also get to complete trust in your abilities through that 10,000 hours theory. If something becomes second nature, you'll be able to sustain flow and expansion no matter how difficult the task is.

Expansion is what distinguishes the ordinary from the extraordinary. People think it's mental discipline, but that's misleading. Any mental discipline that puts you into contraction—beating yourself up, high stakes, thinking you just need to will yourself to push harder—leaks into the moments when it counts and can crack you. I see it as the mental mastery of how to get your body into expansion. Think about your own moments of flow state. Recall the moments you received your most creative ideas and inspiration. What were you doing and how did you *feel*? Were you in expansion? Imagine what would be possible if you lived and operated from expansion and knew how to get yourself back into this state whenever you chose.

This also explains why I've seen some people who are on the verge of becoming tapped in lose connection when they get attached to a specific set of steps or ritual. The rigidity of the prescription or the chasing contracts them, and they lose access. If they're put on the spot, the pressure of being tested sets them into contraction, which blocks their access. For those of you who are becoming tapped in, keep trusting, keep staying in expansion, and you'll begin stabilizing your newfound access.

To see where else this framework fit, I looked up the most well-known quotes. Some famous people have worked *really hard* to succeed and their quotes will be about working hard. If you want to work harder, follow their advice. Working in contraction feels like hard work. Working in expansion feels like play. If you'd like to make quantum leaps, look up quotes from geniuses, visionaries, and artists, and see what wisdom can be simplified into contraction vs. expansion. Here are a few examples:

Working in contraction feels like hard work. Working in expansion feels like play.

"Your time is limited, so don't waste it living someone else's life. Don't be trapped by dogma—which is living with the results of other people's thinking."—Steve Jobs[43]

Don't try to be someone else (that's contraction). If you limit yourself to the beliefs and expectations of 94.7, you will be limited to ordinary results.

"If life were predictable it would cease to be life, and be without flavor."—Eleanor Roosevelt[44]

Contraction is trying to predict and control life. The zest of life is found in opening yourself to the possibilities found only in expansion.

"If you look at what you have in life, you'll always have more. If you look at what you don't have in life, you'll never have enough."—Oprah Winfrey[45]

Focusing on what you do have creates expansion—you'll always have more expansion. If you look at what you don't have, you'll create contraction, which leads to more contraction.

"If you set your goals ridiculously high and it's a failure, you will fail above everyone else's success."—James Cameron[46]

What comes of expansion is still a quantum leap above what comes from contraction.

"The greatest glory in living lies not in never falling, but in rising every time we fall."—Nelson Mandela[47]

The greatest expansion comes not from never being in contraction, but in getting back into expansion every time you get knocked into contraction.

Try this with some of your own favorite quotes, and you'll be surprised how often you see expansion and contraction expressed in their wisdom.

3 STAGES OF LEGACY BUILDING

What I've observed in classmates, friends, and clients is that everyone is in one of three stages of their journey.

Stage 1

This is the stage where you experience the most contraction. It's about proving something—wanting to go from nobody to somebody. "Do I matter?" is what you want to know in this first stage. Establishing you're smart, worthy, lovable, good, important, and valuable drives achieving and striving here. If you can't prove this, you fear rejection. Fear shapes your personality, behaviors, goals, and things you do and don't do.

Stage 2

In the second stage, contraction relaxes as you learn that people would actually pay you for your natural talents and gifts—to be yourself in your zone of genius. You realize, "I do matter!" You begin to live more from expansion than contraction in this second stage.

You may still enjoy some validation, approval, and applause to feel good in this stage.

Stage 3

In the final stage, you say, "Now I want to work on something that matters." You want to use your gifts for good and focus on your contribution to the world. The question becomes, "What matters to me?" vs. "What do I get applause for?" or "What am I still trying to prove?" What you want, what brings you aliveness, and what humanity needs begin to intersect in stage three.

You go from living and working from the space of "Do I matter?" (phase 1: wound) to "I DO matter!" (phase 2: gift) to "I want to work on something that matters" (phase 3: contribution).

What stage are you currently in?

For most, it takes their whole life and career to enter stage three. Now that you know how to ride contraction into expansion, you can enter stage three whenever you decide to. These are not binary states; these are layers that get peeled back like an onion. As your nervous system unravels, you can peel back deeper and deeper layers. You continue unfurling by processing your emotions and sensations. It's key to stay present and engaged with feeling whatever arises so you can go further, peeling back more layers each time.

The challenge is that when our nervous system is tight and we're in contraction, we don't see the places we're lying to *ourselves*. Here are a few examples of questions that are simple to ask, but not easy to answer:

- Are you staying in a job you've convinced yourself you have to stay in to feel financially secure?
- Are you staying in a relationship because you've convinced yourself it's best for all involved?
- How often do you talk yourself into doing things you don't want to do?
- How often do you talk yourself out of things you want to do?
- Do you mentally justify why you're not listening to your heart?

- Do you avoid uncomfortable conversations because you don't want to make someone feel bad?
- Do you keep yourself busy, never making enough time to slow down and face any uncomfortable feelings below the surface?
- Where are you letting what you get approval, applause, and validation for shape who you are and what you do?
- Do you value safety over truth?
- Do you pretend not to know the answers to these questions?

Taking an honest look at where you override your truth for safety will give you insight into the places you may be lying to yourself.

When we stand in truth, we stand in expansion and life appears to flow. There's a coherent resonance and clarity that rings from truth. Author Caroline Myss said, "There is another altitude to life, and the air is sweet."[48] When there are places within ourselves we're uncomfortable going, we seek to control the world, people, and circumstances to keep it from triggering those parts of us. Can we own our contractions, all our parts, and not be horrified by our shadow?

When there is no longer any place you're unwilling to feel and face, you can trust yourself.

From what I've seen, we all have narcissistic qualities. The ones who fear their darkness the most, unwilling to feel their contractions, are the most narcissistic. They struggle to feel others' emotions because they haven't yet acknowledged their own. Bring your full and honest awareness to your contractions. A shift in your inner acceptance activates a far more expanded consciousness. When there is no longer any place you're unwilling to feel and face, you can trust yourself.

When you catch your ego judging or feeling superior, you can say, "A part of me is feeling judgmental, and that's okay, I accept all of me." This acceptance allows you to stay curious and explore this part of you that likes to judge. It allows you to see your own game more clearly because while shame keeps your game in your blind spot, acceptance enables you to more easily tell yourself the truth.

Remember, your shadow is merely the lens you have on reality when you're in contraction. Acceptance leads to expansion, which brings your shadow out of the dark.

Collectively we now understand that hurt people hurt people. Wound-up nervous systems act from contraction. Do not make any decision or take any action from there. Contraction creates further contraction. The only thing to do in this state is *feel* it to release it. Expansion is who we are once we release our contractions. Get back into expansion and think and act from there.

When you are unwilling to do the work of processing your emotions and sensations and uncoiling your nervous system, you will struggle to stay with a viewpoint you disagree with or do not understand. You'll quickly enter binary, black-and-white thinking and judgment, and have difficulty letting in more information. The loss of control and fear of the unknown can be so uncomfortable that you'd rather create a false sense of certainty.

It comes down to how honest you are with yourself. What is your relationship to truth? Do you avoid looking at hard or uncomfortable things? Do you stay in confusion or ambiguity to avoid facing it? Do you downplay how bad things are, or how much you want things to change? Do you fear how the truth will change your life? Can you stand in your truth without knowing whether you'll be met?[49]

Our body loves our honesty. It contracts when we lie to ourselves and try to override what it feels, and it expands even when it hears, "I'm in so much pain, I don't know how to make it stop!" The truth softens the edges of reality creating an opening for something new to happen. I see many people who are stuck in unfavorable circumstances while they deny the truth of how they feel about it. "I'm fine" or "it's not that bad," they say, and they usually add some mental justification for tolerating it.

Here is your ninth unlearning: *It's not until we admit to ourselves how much pain we're in that we can access sufficient energy to say, "Enough!" and create a new reality.*

Do not regulate the pain out of existence or you'll be stuck forever. Don't explain away the pain either. Feel it. The quality of your life is determined by your relationship to discomfort. Your freedom comes not from avoiding contraction (and living in a golden cage), but in knowing how to transmute any contraction into expansion. As you expand your nervous system, you can handle more uncertainty, step outside your comfort zone, and see and hold deeper levels of truth. Your nervous system dictates your bandwidth for information, the main limiter for how much of reality you can perceive.

What our world needs now more than ever are people willing to do the work of unraveling their nervous system so they can expand their bandwidth to hold more perspectives, to look deeper, and be in the diversity of beliefs, people, and life. When our bandwidth is narrow, we feel separate. We fall into an "Us vs. Them" thinking, Drama Triangle[50], and fear what is different. When our bandwidth is expanded, we feel interconnected, one with all, and are inspired by what is different. This is why I believe one of the most commonly reported experiences of participants in a medicine journey is unity consciousness: *"I felt how we're all one."*

You may notice as you move from stage one to stage two, and even stage three, there are some parts of you (layers of you) that will still revisit proving yourself and still wonder about applause. That's okay. You'll notice the volume on these parts turning down. Your greatest expansion will come as you dissolve these parts of yourself. I've found this to be true as I surrender my personal agenda to what is in the best and highest interest of all. As soon as you *must* have something happen and attach to it tightly, you're in contraction. The tighter you hold onto anything (an opinion, person, goal, identity, or object) the more it contracts you.[51] You can hold an expectation without being attached to it. Do not become an unconscious victim to your own expectations.

Every time I dream a new dream, have a new vision, or visualize a new destiny to manifest, I do not hold it tightly. I do not grip it with the contractive energy of, *"This has to happen."* Instead, I notice and release any anxiety I have about it. I hold it with the exciting and expansive energy of, "May this happen or something *even better* for the best and highest of all. May I remove my personal agenda. May I impact millions and billions of lives anonymously. May I be willing to sacrifice my own significance for the best and highest of all." I come from here as I go after what I want. I feel both passionate desire and surrender at the same time. This is how I dissolve the parts of me that may be consciously and unconsciously making it about me, holding a personal agenda, or wanting validation or applause, which all create contraction. In expansion, applause is nice and can create even more expansion, but *needing applause* and letting that influence my actions creates contraction. Instead, I surrender into expansion as I hold my vision for what I want to see happen.

MANIFESTING FROM EXPANSION

You can struggle linearly to create from contraction but you cannot make quantum leaps with ease and grace from contraction. Trying to *force things* creates contraction. Life is not about pushing. Many spiritual teachers and books (such as *Think and Grow Rich, The Law of Attraction, The Secret, The Power of the Subconscious Mind*) talk about manifesting.

> **Here is your tenth unlearning:** *You can't manifest anything you want from contraction.*

It simply doesn't work. You need your body—where your subconscious lives—to be in alignment with your vision. Mindset work alone is not sufficient. *This is not a mindset book.* You may mentally want something, but your subconscious will resist it if it's holding the parts that don't believe you can have it or don't believe you deserve it. Once you've learned how to put yourself into expansion by removing areas of contraction, you can manifest your visions in no time.

One of my clients, George Ruan, co-founder and CEO of Honey, started working with me on August 14, 2018, when his company was valued at $700M, with a little more than one hundred employees. We worked on his leadership skills, which included scaling his impact, operationalizing his culture's values, and creating a company vision to inspire his teams. We worked on removing key areas of contraction so that he could live from peak performance. When he started this work, he had weekly headaches, which he called brain fog, that would last for days. He slept poorly and was constantly hypervigilant. His inner critic and discontent were his fuel, and he held all sorts of beliefs that kept him in contraction. He also said that while he had every-thing he ever wanted, "a perfect life," he didn't feel happy. His mental model and conditioned contraction were in the way of his fulfillment. Week to week, we excavated all his old ways of being, beliefs, and perceptions as they showed up in the challenges he brought to each call. Every week we updated his operating system, upgraded his lens on reality, and expanded his consciousness.

Then on July 19, 2019, I asked George to start his mornings with a walking meditation visualizing his meeting with PayPal's engi-neers. This wasn't a normal meditation. I was showing George what's possible when he puts himself into expansion. I asked him to walk to his office every morning with confidence, a pep in his step, proud of what his company built, as he imagined with all five senses his meeting with the PayPal engineering team going incredibly well and how impressed they would be by what Honey had built. After three weeks of this morning walking meditation, PayPal offered to acquire Honey. The offer came as a complete surprise. George had no plans to sell. He expected to take his company public. Through a process of tracking contraction and expansion in George's system, we determined whether or not to sell his company and at what price. By August 18, 2019, after Honey rejected their first offer, PayPal came back with the offer to acquire the company for $4B, which George accepted. When I eventually shared with George how his daily morning visualization of this PayPal meeting from a place of expansion manifested his acquisition offer, he responded, "So we live in a simulation."

Let me tell you how I manifested George. I was headed to Greece to celebrate my thirty-first birthday, and before I took off, I set the intention of finding my dream clients on this trip. I thought I may meet them on the plane or something. Then in Mykonos, I happened to end up in a house with George who was there as a guest of a mutual friend. He said I stood out from the coaches he's worked with, so he was curious to try a session. Today, he's still a client, and plans to bring me on for all future endeavors.

When I began my work with Honey, I visualized them being an anchor client success story, my first example of a multibillion-dollar exit. I put a picture up of the Honey founders above my work desk with text stating this vision, and within one year of our work together, it was realized.

These are the results of my clients without my telling them, "This is called manifesting." I watch my language as I don't want to turn off these skeptical engineers and scientists. I make it sound *practical, not magical.* No belief required. They're doing what I share in this book and they're bending reality. They don't even need to understand why it works to get results. This is how I can be tool and modality agnostic. Every client receives custom advising.

Here is another fun manifesting story. When people ask me why I mainly work with entrepreneurs, I tell them that I want to find and support the Elon Musks of the world, the visionaries who are steering humanity toward its highest destiny. In March 2019, I was invited to Cuba by my Harvard Business School classmate Megumi Gordon and her husband, Michael Laverty, who run a travel company focusing on trips to Cuba. I'd never been to Cuba and they said it would be a good opportunity to see if I might want to run my leadership retreats there. They were hosting an event for about a hundred people and invited me to join as their guest. I showed up by myself, fully open to the experience.

The way I keep myself in expansion during these kinds of events with strangers is I remind myself to trust that whatever is meant to happen will happen, in the best and highest of all. Surrendering through trust puts you into a deep pool of expansion. I'm not sure it even matters whether it's true, as long as what you tell yourself puts you into expansion. On the third evening of my Cuba adventure, I met a lovely, smart, and engaging woman named Natasha. We talked for an hour about her journey into self-development and the books I'd recommend. At the end of our conversation she said, "My husband should really work with you." I asked her, 'Is your husband an entrepreneur?' She said, "Not right now, he's figuring it out. Would you still speak to him?" I enjoyed my conversation with her so I said, "Yes, of course, I'll see how I can help."

On the day the emails got shared from that 100-person event, I immediately received an email from Peter Rive, Natasha's husband. I only googled his name after our initial call and in the first result, I saw that he's Elon Musk's cousin and he cofounded SolarCity, which was acquired by Tesla for $2.6B. I didn't even know that such a person was at the event. I'm no longer surprised when things like this happen to me or my clients, but I'm always in awe.

If you choose to cultivate expansion in your nervous system, you will be endlessly amazed by the results you get in every area of your life. The experience of synchronicity, receiving downloads, manifesting your visions, and flow state, what athletes call "in the zone"—all of this is available to you in expansion, the state required to bend reality. The universe is the most epic scavenger hunt and finding this book is *your* first clue.

HOW DO YOU MANIFEST FROM EXPANSION?

Imagine what feels expansive to you and let that be your only guiding light. As you focus on thoughts that feel expansive, you will always be in expansion. If contraction creeps in when you think a thought you'd like to believe, feel the contraction fully to release it. You cannot feel one way and then try to override the feeling by repeating some affirmation. If you hold shame and tell yourself, "I'm amazing!" it will feel like you're lying to yourself and your affirmations will not pass your own bullshit detector. Feel the shame fully until it transmutes. Then think the expansive thought and feel the expansion in your body.

Make sure your whole body—every finger, toe, and muscle—is relaxed. Feel your chest area soften. Completely immersed, let yourself lose awareness of yourself and your surroundings. Imagine yourself in your vision, looking out from your own eyes onto everything around you. Visualize with your mind's eye, and engage all five senses, so that it comes so alive you can taste it. Feel the elevated emotion and resonance as if it's all happening in this very moment. Imagine you have what you are envisioning: health, wealth, whatever it is you're picturing, and feel healthy, wealthy. Feel the emotion that resonates with your vision. Give your body the experience of having what you want, as if it's already happened.

Let the emotions flow through your open heart. Feel your mind and heart melding together as they play with this vision. And then *let it go.* Don't wrinkle your forehead and forcefully focus because that will put you into contraction. Focus your attention and intention on what you want from a place of expansion. Do not let any old beliefs get in the way. Notice any feelings of inadequacy, disbelief, or doubt that come up as they only create contraction. Notice any fear or judgment, "Do I deserve that?" because all of this creates contraction. Feel those contractions completely to release them.

5th CODE TO BENDING REALITY
Feel your vision coming true from a place of expansion.

If you fall into contraction, you will repel what you want. If you maintain expansion as you visualize what you want, you'll leap octaves up into expansion. From here, you can warp the fabric of spacetime and manifest what you want or something *even* better.

DON'T WAIT FOR THE HOW

There is a high degree of indifference, boredom, and compromise on the planet created by people who are not doing what they would truly love to be doing. Richard Rudd shares that most first learn this in school; they learn to associate work with boredom and effort instead of enjoyment and enthusiasm. This contagious compromise becomes a habit, tames their spirit, and takes them further away from their full potential.[52] As adults, they make all sorts of excuses for not pursuing what they want, and once that excuse isn't true anymore, they find another one.

"Now's not a good time, I need to make a certain amount of money first."
"Now's not a good time, I'm going to start planning to have a family."
"Now's not a good time, I just had a baby."
"Now's not a good time, my partner is going up for a big promotion."
"Now's not a good time, the world is in a lot of uncertainty."
"Now's not a good time, my kids need me."

It has nothing to do with time. It has everything to do with making yourself a victim of fear. *Feel* whatever is in the way of your dream. Do not downplay how much you want your dream. Let yourself truly feel what it stirs in your heart. The moment you claim your dreams, you'll find yourself at the right place at the right time.

The moment you claim your dreams, you'll find yourself at the right place at the right time.

Things happen in no time at all. Once you own your dream, you activate your path:[53] the stepping-stones reveal themselves to you one by one. Your path only requires you to take the next step that's visible to you, trusting the one after that will appear just in time. Do not wait for the how. The how will not be revealed to you until you're walking toward your dream. You create your path as you walk it.

The how is always way more magical than the mind could have planned. I see it as a scavenger hunt, where each time I take bold action toward my dream, I receive the next clue. You cannot just think and feel your dream, you must also take aligned action toward it. The more you follow your heart, the easier it gets to listen to it. You enter a new current. Momentum builds. You expand exponentially when you listen. When you deny your heart, you contract and wear down your health. Your mind tends to confirm later what the heart already knows. Follow your heart to find your destiny.

When we are in our truth, we are expanded and in flow. When we're not in truth, we struggle and are taught to expect struggle. We almost do not trust what comes easily to us. We usually undervalue our natural gifts and talents because of this. In other words, we often undervalue our natural self and go off striving. The challenge is that there are so many mental justifications, such as, "But I *have* to do this in order to make a good living" to override the body's contraction that most cannot tell how they're lying to themselves. Their mental model justifies their worldview and becomes self-fulfilling. If they expect "no pain, no gain," then they'll have plenty of where that came from.

This is *your* life. Everyone and everything benefits from you *living* it. Everyone and everything suffers from you making excuses for not living it. The repression of your dreams cuts you off from your life force energy and puts you in a sleepy state of indifference, compromise, and boredom or in a reactive state of anger, resentment, and denial. In other words, it puts you in contraction. Your dreams are sacred. Keep them close and nurture them. You must believe in them while giving them space to grow and turn out differently than you imagined. If you hold your dreams tightly, attached to how they take form, then you will limit their possibilities to your narrow concepts. Follow your dreams from a place of expansion.

My clients and I create new dreams on a daily, weekly, monthly, quarterly, and annual basis. We spend time visioning clearly before we take any action. We check for congruence in beliefs, emotions, and imagination. From here, we take action.

We each have a dream within us that only we can bring to life, and we're here to realize it.

EXERCISE: MAKE MANIFEST

You may be so used to compromising that you don't even notice when you're doing it. Open yourself to the highest possibilities for your life. What dreams are you aware of? What dreams have you put on hold? What does your life look like in your wildest dreams? Feel what it stirs in your heart.

Close your eyes and imagine the dream or goal you want to realize. Picture it with rich detail as if it's happening in this present moment. What do you see? Experience it with all five senses and let it come so alive like you can almost taste it. Feel it come true from a place of expansion.

CHAPTER 10

How to Live from Expansion in Everyday Life

TO MOVE TOWARD EXPANSION, FOCUS YOUR ATTEN-tion on what you want to happen, and move toward your vision. Many people unconsciously operate and live from a place of avoiding what they don't want, what they're scared will happen, which keeps them operating from contraction and reaction vs. expansion and creation. They are running away from contraction vs. moving toward expansion. Their attention is on the problem, not the solution. Keep your attention on expansion; living there enhances every aspect of your life from your physical body to your relationships to your finances.

EVERYDAY EXPANSION
To help you understand what living in expansion means, let's look at a few specific areas and explore the difference between operating from expansion vs. contraction.

Health and Fitness

There are two ways of going about having the body you want. You can either operate from contraction by avoiding what you don't want (weight gain). Or you can operate from expansion by moving toward what you do want (a healthy fit body).

If you're in contraction focused on avoiding weight gain, you may try a diet and then get hard on yourself when you cheat on your diet. You may exercise a lot, or try all sorts of weight loss pills, potions, and lotions. You may even become a drill sergeant about your food and exercise, and in some cases, develop an unhealthy eating disorder. When you look in the mirror, you're hard on yourself, focusing on what you don't like and how you wished you looked different. You look at other bodies for comparison and judge yours. You feel like you perpetually want to lose weight. You think about your weight multiple times a day. You beat yourself up for eating things you enjoy, and you may end up binge eating in reaction to depriving yourself. Can you feel how much contraction there is behind this mode?

Now let's look at what coming from expansion and moving toward a healthy, fit body looks like. You may still choose to eat healthy foods, but it'll be coming from empowerment, a sense of self-love. You're taking care of yourself vs. judging, shaming, and being critical of yourself. Instead of looking at the menu in terms of "what I can't have/what I'm depriving myself of," you'll be looking for tasty foods that nourish your body and feel good to digest. You'll choose places that have lots of those options. In expansion, you're more attuned to trusting what your body naturally craves and less likely to overeat or forget to eat. You notice the foods your body likes, and the ones that make you crash or that don't sit well in your stomach. You choose exercises that are fun for you. If you hate running, you won't make yourself run. You'll play tennis or take a dance class. Maybe you'll decide to walk more places and enjoy podcasts and audiobooks while you move your body. When you skip a workout, you won't judge and criticize yourself. You'll just get back on it tomorrow. When you eat something you love, you don't sit there regretting it after, feeling guilty, immediately feeling contracted. When you feel good and expansive, everything is easier, including making healthier choices that are self-supporting.

If you haven't realized it yet, you don't need an internalized parent or drill sergeant to whip you into shape. In fact, that only creates more contraction, and the goal of this book is to guide you toward expansion. In expansion, you create healthier sustainable changes such as finding that gym class you enjoy, that trainer you love, or you start cooking more. When you look in the mirror from a place of expansion, you see yourself through loving eyes and focus on your beauty. You do not hold your routines and healthy habits like prescriptions. Holding anything that tightly creates contraction. Instead, you keep them for as long as they serve you and allow yourself to fluidly switch things up.

Which scenario do you connect with? What parts of you are relating to your body from a place of contraction vs. expansion?

> **In expansion, you have conscious choice. In contraction, you have an unconscious reaction.**

The next time you're contemplating a decision, list the reasons for your choice and see how many of them are moving you *toward* expansion vs. *away from* contraction. Make sure you're driven toward the direction of expansion (a healthy, fit body), not away from contraction (weight gain). Making a business decision? Notice if your reasons are moving you toward your vision vs. away from your fear of competitors, loss of revenue, or a damaged brand. Is your decision coming from expansion or contraction? In expansion, you have conscious choice. In contraction, you have an unconscious reaction.

Communication

Imagine you and your romantic partner have dinner plans after a long day at work. You're both tired and your nervous systems are tense from the work week. You're both in contraction. You feel disappointed that your romantic partner showed up late to dinner again, leaving you waiting for 30 minutes alone and hungry at the restaurant. When your partner arrives, your tone, body language, and eyes convey your feelings. You say, "You're late again."

In contraction, your romantic partner feels attacked, and goes into binary thinking: *"Am I right or wrong?" "Am I a good or bad partner?"* There's a feeling of shame and defense as they say, "I'm sorry. I couldn't help it. You know how work is. I tried to get out as soon as I could, and then there was unexpected traffic from a car accident." You reply, *"This happens all the time"* and create even more shame. Now they're defending themselves, justifying all the times, and asking you to be understanding.

In contraction, your partner unconsciously feels like if your pain is acknowledged fully, then they're a bad partner. You feel uncared for, your attempt at date night is ruined and you blame it on your partner for showing up late.

Now imagine the same scenario except that one or both of you is in expansion. Your nervous system is relaxed, and you can see beyond the "good/bad" or "right/wrong" polarity of contraction. When your romantic partner shows up 30 minutes late, you say, "I'm really hungry, let's try to put in our order." Your partner gets it and starts scanning the menu. You put in your food order, and then you say, "I've been waiting here hungry for 30 minutes and it doesn't feel good." Your romantic partner says, "Yes, I'm sorry. I feel awful that you were sitting here hungry for 30 minutes waiting for me. It's one of the things I really don't like about my job. It's so unpredictable. And of course, it didn't help that there was unusual traffic from a car accident."

In expansion, you respond truthfully, "Yes, I wish there was something you could do or say to make sure you can get out of the office when you need to. When you show up late, it makes me feel like I'm less important to you than work. And I'd like to feel more important to you than work." In expansion, your partner doesn't make this about being good/bad, right/wrong, it's not an either/or conversation. Your partner responds, "You *are* more important to me than work, and I can see how showing up late could make you feel that way. I'm going to make a point of telling my team at the start of the day that I need to be out at 7 p.m. sharp to make our date night." You smile, feeling heard and cared for, and your partner smiles, grateful that you're so understanding. You have a game plan for how to improve the situation and your food arrives.

Which scenario can you see yourself in? In your romantic partnership, are you coming from a lens of contraction or expansion?

You can go to therapy and learn scripts for what to say and how to say it, but it will feel like a struggle as long as your nervous systems are wound up and you're in contraction. No matter what words come out of your mouth, people will feel the tone, whether you're coming from contraction or expansion. In expansion there's space for "Yes, and" thinking vs. "either/or" thinking. There's room for "I was well intentioned *and* it had a negative impact" vs. "I was well intentioned, so I wasn't wrong." There's room for "I know this may not be true, but this is the story I had about what was going on." It's way easier to listen from here. In expansion, it's not about good/bad, right/wrong, any judgment, or what it

The best thing you can do for anyone you love is cultivate expansion.

says about you; it's about what's true for each of you, and expansion gives you access to more of reality and more of what's true.

The best thing you can do for anyone you love is to cultivate expansion. The worst thing you can do is to be in contraction and then expect them to change it or ask *them* to change when there is nothing that anybody else can do to release your contraction. Do not make anyone else responsible for transmuting your contraction and do not make yourself responsible for transmuting another's contraction. That's codependent behavior. Own, feel, and release your own contractions. Practice interdependence by recognizing the impact you have on one another. Words, choices, and actions that come of contraction create more contraction. Words, choices, and actions that come of expansion create more expansion.

Masculinity and Femininity

We all have both masculinity and femininity, yin and yang, within us so this is a gender-neutral topic. I believe that the world to date has experienced both masculine and feminine in contraction. Now we're seeing the rise of healthy masculinity and healthy femininity in expansion, and what's possible for healthy integration and union of the masculine and feminine.

When the masculine in anyone is in contraction, it's quick to feel like a failure. In contraction, it feels shame. It says, *"What does this say about me? I'm not smart enough, strong enough, good enough. I don't have what it takes."* Shame, sadness, and fear all easily turn into anger when the masculine is in contraction. Anger can easily turn into aggression.

When the feminine is in contraction, the heart becomes guarded. A wall goes up to protect itself from hurt. The feminine becomes closed off and disconnected from its sensations and emotions. In contraction, the feminine is quick to feel unloved. Its shame sounds like: *"Am I lovable? Am I deserving of love? Am I ___enough to be loved?"* Anger can easily turn into sadness and withdrawal. Shame, fear, and hurt all easily turn into sadness when the feminine is in contraction.

When the masculine is in expansion, it becomes grounded, pure awareness, like a big container that can hold and witness it all. It focuses on and quantifies the outcome and curiously looks for what happened so it can learn and improve the result. The masculine holds space for the emotions to be felt like the riverbed providing structure to the river.

When the feminine is in expansion, it becomes an open heart that can feel and stay open no matter what flows through it. Its senses are enlivened. It looks at the result and wants to improve the quality by envisioning a new dream for its potential. The feminine is a river and allows all its emotions to flow freely. It becomes a master at processing and being *with* its hurt, fear, sadness, anger— all of it. It can feel and stand in the fire of its raw emotion and express without overreacting or underreacting. From this place of truth, the feminine magnetizes.

Which parts of your masculine and feminine are in contraction or expansion? A vision that I have for every gender is for both their masculine and feminine parts to be in expansion.

Money

In contraction, you may believe the more money you make, the more worthy you are. You may feel that your identity is wrapped up in owning more things. The more you acquire, the more you feel you need to protect what you own. You may feel like there's never enough of it, and not realize when you are underearning or unconsciously spending. You may feel possessive of money, afraid of spending it. You need to acquire more and more of it to feel safe. You may believe you have to work harder to make more money, or you may feel trapped in a job you hate that drains you and believe you're stuck in order to survive. Money feels zero-sum. There's a finite amount of it to go around.

You may even resist money, thinking it is the root of all evil and you therefore avoid receiving it. You may be vague about how much you want to make, save, and owe. These are all ways we relate to money from contraction.

In expansion, you feel abundant, and money is a byproduct of you creating in expansion. You can identify the beliefs of scarcity, fear, and contraction you learned directly and indirectly from how your parents relate to money. You see how if you believe you have to work 24/7 to make money, then you will. If you believe you have to put making money above your hobbies, friends, and family to survive, you will. You see how if you aren't making enough money, you'll believe you have to work harder. Reality conforms to your worldview. You see how what you perceive becomes reality and so you quickly flip the script on your beliefs. You catch yourself when you say, "I can't ..." and start believing you can.

This happens at the sensation level, where your body feels expansive about your new beliefs. The new beliefs feel resonant in your body. You feel expansive both making and spending money. When you pay a bill, instead of feeling contractive, you feel grateful that you got to enjoy the goods or service you experienced. Instead of placing value on money, you place value on you—the creator and source of value—and your process of creation.[54] You value your unique gifts and money flows easily to you.

You can make money the hard way in contraction or you can make money the easy way in expansion. The difference of outcomes between contraction and expansion explains what many perceive as "luck." You can look over at someone who doesn't appear to be any more capable, intelligent, or deserving than you are and watch them take a chance on a new idea, job, or opportunity, and see them succeed. "They're lucky," you say. I say, "They must have believed and trusted enough to access expansion.

"They're lucky," you say. I say, "They must have believed and trusted enough to access expansion."

They must've connected to their values, vision, purpose, passion, and the fun they had going after it enough to give them access to expansion." This is the recipe for luck!

Instead of using money to change your circumstances, use it to expand your consciousness by investing time, money, and energy into things that expand you. My favorite money self-development books are *Think and Grow Rich* by Napoleon Hill, *The Energy of Money* by Maria Nemeth, and *You're a Badass at Making Money* by Jen Sincero. Notice what contractive beliefs you have about money and what expansive beliefs you have about money. How can you turn all your money beliefs of contraction into beliefs of expansion?

LOVE AND RELATIONSHIPS

Romantic relationships often feel so wonderful at the beginning during the honeymoon period. *This person makes me feel so expansive!* you think. Then if they do or say the wrong thing, the contractive impact on you is far greater than their intention. You might think, *I'm not important. I'm not good enough. I'm not _____ (successful, smart, beautiful, kind, providing, protecting, man) enough.* In contraction, you bring all your unexamined fears, insecurities, and shame into the relationship. You may think, *Do I matter? Am I good enough? Am I deserving?* You hope your partner makes you feel all the expansive things about yourself that you haven't yet learned to feel about yourself independently.

Then with everything your romantic partner does and says—or doesn't do or say—you make it mean something about *you*. In contraction, it's like there are all these little landmines that neither of you realize are there representing old stories, fears, programming, shame, and insecurities. Until one gets stepped on, you have *no* idea that they're there. You don't realize that you've projected all your own unexamined beliefs onto your romantic partner, putting your worst inner critic into their mind, assuming they're thinking your own contractive thoughts about you, and you're looking for confirmation in their words and actions. You're so focused on whether or not your partner is seeing you all the ways you're afraid are true about you, that you don't realize that it's all a reflection of your own unexamined views of yourself.

In contraction, any qualities you see in your partner that you have not yet learned to accept within yourself will bring your harshest judgment. Your arguments lead to what John Gottman[55] calls the Four Horsemen: Criticism, Defensiveness, Contempt, and Stonewalling. Both of you are left feeling misunderstood, disconnected, and more alone. You feel unloved, unheard, and unseen. Your fears bring out the worst in you, and then you've made them self-fulfilling.

Let's look at what love looks like in expansion. You feel open, trusting, and worthy. You don't make your partner's words or actions mean anything about you. If they say and do nice things, you feel even more expansive, but you're not relying on them to get you out of contraction and into expansion with their words or actions. You know that is nobody's job but your own. When you're in expansion, you're not in fight-or-flight mode, wondering if you're going to lose love or be abandoned. If they do or say something hurtful, you tell them what you need and you trust that they'll do their best to meet you. If they can't, and it's important to you, then you can tell them, "This doesn't work for me." If your partner truly can't or won't for whatever reason, and it is a deal-breaker for you, you don't sacrifice your truth and resent your partner. You also don't try to change them or make them feel wrong until they change. You find a solution that works for the both of you or you move on.

In expansion, you see that you need to love and accept someone first in order to understand them. You also realize that growth can only happen when one feels safe, and it happens much more quickly if they're not being judged. Mistakes are okay. You can feel bad for the impact you had without it turning into shame, self-judgment, and self-hate, which makes it easier to choose differently in the future. There's acceptance for things looking messy and imperfect as you each grow and try things outside your comfort zone. This acceptance leads to less denial, justification, anger, shame, or guilt. The more love, acceptance, and understanding exist, the easier it is to grow.

When there is conflict, you can each own your part because when you're in expansion you realize that you co-create everything in a relationship. You can own your apology and ask for what you can do to clean it up and do better in the future. Whether it's not speaking up sooner or not being proud of how you reacted, there's always a part to own. Responsibility is not zero-sum. You don't need to divide up whose fault it is, where the more it's your fault, the less it's their fault or vice versa. In expansion, it's not about whose fault it is, who is right or wrong, good or bad. Instead, you have access to solutions. You can be creative with what to do even if the conversation is, "I don't think we'll ever agree on this, so what do we do given that?"

The more love, acceptance, and understanding exist, the easier it is to grow.

In expansion, there's safety and space for truth and honesty. You keep your commitments to each other since you realize that's the foundation for trust and trust sustains expansion. You both understand that trust starts with your relationship with yourself—with your ability to trust your own word, keep promises to yourself, and speak up for yourself. As soon as you are aware that you cannot honor your commitments, you speak up and see what you can do to recover. You do not lie to yourself, to each other, or about each other. You understand that all lies create invisible walls, giving the lies a life of their own that create contraction ripples throughout the relationship.

In expansion, there is nothing you're unwilling to see, nothing from past or present you're unwilling to acknowledge or be with. However messy the truth is, you honor authenticity and honesty. You even tell the truth on each other, calling each other forward, "Is that your truth? Or is it your old story making you believe that?" You lovingly wake each other up when either of you goes unconscious. Instead of holding someone statically in judgment with comments such as, *"You always _____. You'll never change,"* there's a spacious invitation for growth and trust that they're fully capable of meeting you. You see them as a whole, conscious being with choice. Not as a broken, less-good version of you.

When it comes to sharing your hurt or disappointment, it's not a confrontation, accusation, blame, judgment, or giving a piece of your mind. It's the discernment of noticing when you're accusing and assuming someone's intent vs. sharing what is felt in your experience, speaking only to the impact. The more you come to value yourself, your being, and your experience, the easier it is to recognize and feel the impact on you without minimizing, normalizing, or rationalizing it away. You stand up for yourself, expressing yourself clearly and kindly. You know that this is how you keep your body feeling safe, your nervous system calm because it trusts you have its back.

You know that any resentment is a sign that you've abandoned yourself by not speaking up sooner or choosing to leave the relationship if you truly need something that cannot be given in this relationship. In expansion, you're attuned to your body so you can tell if a *Yes* is a true resounding Yes in the body, and you can feel your *No*, and know that your No is an act of self-respect. You don't make the other's *Yes* or *No* mean something about you. You can understand each other's Yes and No and collaborate to find a mutual Yes. With your nervous systems unraveled, seeing reality more clearly, you can say, "I'm a 90 percent yes to that plan. To get me to 100 percent, can we go on a cooler day?" In expansion, there's clearer communication, more accurate information exchanged and access to the field of infinite possibilities and probabilities.

In expansion, you do not repress, hide, or deny parts of yourself to be loved or validated. You do not look to fix, save, or be saved. Since your nervous system is unraveled, you are more connected to your sensations and emotions, so you notice when you feel unsafe. You do not override it. You notice any contraction and allow yourself to be with the contraction. "That hurt my feelings. That triggered my old sense of not feeling like I matter." You go into it, feeling it fully at 100 percent. Perhaps some tears release. The image of your father never being home comes to mind. You feel your stomach tighten up and keep breathing slowly. Then it dissipates and what you felt was released. This all happens in seconds and minutes. It passes as suddenly as it comes on. You then speak up and take whatever action is needed to establish safety.

Your nervous system will allow you to feel as much as its bandwidth can allow in that moment without short-circuiting. As your nervous system continues to relax, and it feels safer feeling more, you will access more feelings that are coming up to be released. So the best way to move through this is to allow yourself to go into the eye of the storm. Feel it fully so you can release as much as you can each time.

In expansion, when you notice the other person upset, hurt, or in contraction, you don't judge them, criticize them, shame them, or avoid them. You also don't enable them, excuse them, or placate them. You first check in with yourself, "Do I feel safe, expansive, well-resourced to support them?" If the answer is *yes*, you ask, "What can I do to support you right now?" or "What do you need right now?" Sometimes they may not know the answer, and that's okay. Just let them know you're there for them. You may simply be with them as they feel through what they're processing. You can do this easily in expansion because you're not making their hurt, upset, or contraction mean something about you, and you're also not making yourself responsible for fixing it.

If you do not feel ready or you feel you're in contraction yourself, you can say, "I need to take a few minutes by myself; can we reconnect in thirty minutes after we've both had a moment to process what happened?" In thirty minutes, you can share what you each would like the other person to understand about what happened. Now there's space for, "I didn't mean to hurt you, but I can see the negative impact my actions had."

There is a lot of space in expansion for responses vs. reactions, for new perspectives, for listening, for new ways of being, new ways of showing up, new solutions, and truth. From here, your romantic partnership becomes a safe place to release old beliefs, stories, triggers, and landmines; it becomes an opportunity to find all the places of contraction and remind each other that *you are not your contractions*. This is what I call conscious partnership. If you both choose, your relationship can be a place to unravel and shed contraction— what is not you. It can be a place for you each to create, express, and experience who you truly are. You stand for each other's essence and help each other rise higher into expansion.

It feels safe to be raw, imperfect, half-baked, messy, real, and truly seen. Not some polished, put-together, perfect being who is acutely conscious because you've done a lot of work on yourself. Rather, you can be vulnerable and make mistakes, and you're able to recover because it feels safe for *all of you*—the parts you love and the parts you hide. While in contraction, there's too much unsafety, criticism, blame, shame, judgment, evaluating, assessing, comparing, projecting, and expecting for intimacy to be built. In expansion, intimacy becomes your default way of connecting.

If you're in contraction reading this, you may be wondering, "But what if I get taken advantage of?" Just because you accept someone and allow them the freedom to be who they are does not mean you have to continue being with them. It just means you stop trying to control or change them to be someone they're not. If who they are doesn't work for you, then it's your responsibility to leave. If you choose to stay with them, stop making them wrong. Allow them the freedom to be their most expanded version of themselves and become the most expanded version of you, and see if your expanded versions still want to be together. When you're expanded, your expansion is no longer conditional upon any person or circumstance being the way you want. You truly want whatever is in the best and highest interest of all. You don't *need* the other person—you *choose* the other person. The parts of you that fear losing love, being alone, wondering if you'll be okay all come from contraction, which want from a person or situation what you haven't learned how to give yourself.

From expansion, you speak your gratitudes freely, expressing everything you appreciate about the other person. When you have an expansive lens on, it's easier to see and focus on what you love about the person. With a contractive lens on, it's easier to see and focus on what you don't love about the person. What you value appreciates, and your partner becomes even more wonderful. You participate in the creation through your witnessing. Do you hold your partner fluidly or statically? The observer shapes the observed. As you see them, so they become.[56] Love grows through expansion and dies through contraction.

The observer shapes the observed. As you see them, so they become.

What lens do you have on in your relationship right now? Have you created a downward spiral of contraction or are you consciously creating an upward spiral of expansion?

« »

I've given you examples of what it looks like to come from contraction vs. expansion in a few universally key areas of our lives. What I've seen is that many books, therapists, coaches, and programs out there will map out scripts, one-pagers, steps, and frameworks on what to do and say, and offer root cause analysis, theories, and research that explain what is happening. But the truth is, none of these will feel accessible to you until you unwind your nervous system to live in expansion. Until then, you can mentally know how you'd like to be and yet still struggle to become it.

While in contraction, you need a lot of rules, to memorize a lot of things, and override a lot of reactions. In expansion, it all comes out as effortlessly as being. Once embodied, there's nothing left to remember. All the rules, behaviors, and "if then" statements of how to handle different situations as a good leader, parent, or partner are created from an expansive consciousness. Teachers hope that if people memorize the ideals and remind themselves to practice them, "think and behave like *this* ... not like *that*," then they, too, will become good leaders, parents, or partners. We need laws because of the actions people take from contraction. In expansion, there is no harm to self or others. If we teach people how to get into expansion, these ways of being will come naturally in all areas of life. It's the difference between adding features to a rotary phone and upgrading to the latest iPhone. However, what's missing is not a technological innovation but an innovation in consciousness.

EXERCISE: CONSCIOUS PARTNERSHIP

What are some of your landmines? Do you have a fear of rejection, being wrong, abandoned, dismissed, unimportant, too much, not enough, unlovable, or not a kind person? Recall the moments you felt most upset with or hurt by your partner, and notice how their words or actions touched this fear. This awareness alone will help de-escalate contraction. It's even better if both of you are aware of each other's landmines.

If you're ready to take your conscious partnership to the next level, I invite you to shed light on the unconscious programming running in your relationship by following this process:

1. Make a list of all the traits (positive and negative) of your parents' relationship or of your caregivers' relationship. The longer the list, the better.

2. Describe how each quality plays out in that relationship, e.g., "Codependent—they do everything together; Affectionate—they hold hands, and kiss in public; Explosive arguments—their disagreements escalate very quickly; Controlling—need things to go their way; Blaming—quick to blame the other and not take responsibility," and so on.

3. Describe how each trait plays out in its unique way in your relationship (past or present).

4. Write down the new conscious agreements you'd like to make around each relationship quality. Examples: "Interdependent—we understand the impact we have on each other and enjoy doing things together and on our own; Affectionate—we like to maintain our connection whether that's through touching or eye gazing; Calm communication—we ask for what we need including sometimes a 30-minute break to clear our heads," and so on.

CHAPTER 11

What to Expect When You're Expanding

EXPANSION IS NOT SOME SELF-SACRIFICING, MONKLIKE path that's not fun but good for you and the planet. This is actually the path of *most* fun because you live and operate from expansion— your essence—what lights *you* up! You get to enjoy yourself. Everyone around you benefits from you being in expansion. I feel as if I'm playing every day, paid well to be myself, and I prioritize cultivating my joy and expansion because that's what enables all the magic in my life. That's what empowers me to show up as the most powerful version of me for the planet. The journey of turning contraction into expansion is the journey of turning pain into power. This is the path from ordinary to extraordinary.

FREEDOM FRIENDS

It's worth mentioning that as you expand your consciousness, taking in more of reality, that you'll notice clearly where someone is at with their bandwidth on reality. You'll be able to see if their perceptions come from a place of contraction or expansion. In fact, chances are you've probably been surrounded by people who remind you of your old contractions—*how you used to view the world.* You may struggle to make your newfound expansion your default way of being as you're triggered by others' contraction-creating judgments from their lens on reality. They may say, "You really think you can do that? Who do you think you are? That seems really hard and too risky. Don't you think you should _____ (settle down, be married already, get a real job, save up for a house, start having kids, and so on)?"

As you stretch yourself outside the comfort zone of 94.7, your body will naturally feel some contraction. Your inner critic and its old beliefs will get louder in an effort to "protect" you by saying, "You're not ready. This isn't going to work. What if you fail? What will people think?" What feels safe is what's familiar. The inner critic's danger alarm will go off as you approach the border of your comfort zone to reach for your biggest dream, your most expanded you.

To make it past the border of your comfort zone, you must break free from the gravitational pull of 94.7. To do that, practice the tools I've shared in this book for ways to release contraction (see page 95) and access expansion (see page 44). Revisit the exercises at the end of the chapters. Consciously choose with whom you surround yourself, especially as you're crossing over into expansion. Get clear on the people in your life who celebrate your expansion, the ones who believe in you even when you don't yet believe in yourself. The people are not just open to your new ways of being, but are inspired by who you're becoming. Do they celebrate your unique expression—you marching to the beat of your own drum—or do they feel nervous or contracted by it? Find allies who help you remember your originality vs. those who want you to conform. Choose friends who give you the freedom to evolve and who do not hold you in a concept or box of limited possibilities.[57] Don't worry if there aren't many of these people in your life right now. You will quickly attract them as you expand.

Get clear on who the people are in your life who are unconsciously contracted and feel threatened by your expansion. These people might compare, judge, envy, resent, criticize, gossip, and get defensive. They may feel attacked by what you do and say that's different from what they do and say. They may worry about your new ways of being and feel they must convince you to see it their way. Seeing how happy and free you are with your new choices may make them question their own choices, especially if they've been following 94.7 and are tired, unhappy, and contracted. The more you get yourself into expansion, the more you're able to avoid taking any of this personally.

These may be good friends, family members, or even a romantic partner. It will be tempting to judge them or feel superior or "more awake" than them, but that'll just put you into contraction and judgment is never silent. Some spiritual masters say judgment (of self and others) weakens your health more than any other thought because you're contracting and winding up your nervous system with each one. This is also why many teach that forgiveness is not for the other person—it's for you. It may be tempting to confront them and point out their contraction. It is not your responsibility to change anyone. Be mindful of putting anyone into more contraction. How receptive are you to change when you're being judged or criticized? Winding up their nervous system even more doesn't help.

When you're in expansion, you cannot help but uplift those with whom you come into contact. Lead by example. Inspire them. Show them another way. Your freedom will be contagious. They may notice, desire, and work to achieve expansion themselves, but you cannot give it to them. Each person is responsible for their own internal state. If you care about their growth, accept them as they are because safety is a prerequisite for growth. Again, this doesn't mean you have to put yourself in situations that create contraction for you. You can try sharing:

"It doesn't feel good when you judge or criticize my decisions."

"Your need to control things to go the way you want makes me feel on edge."

"I am making different choices from you, and I'd appreciate it if you would not make them better or worse just because they're different."

"I notice that when you're in a bad mood, it affects how you treat me and our relationship. It's important to me that we figure out a solution for this."

If you still cannot maintain your expansion around these people, take care of yourself. Do what you need to do. Do not abandon yourself in order to keep someone else in their comfort zone. You must put your nervous system's expansion first. You can ask yourself, "What boundaries do I need to create to protect my expansion?" Do not ignore your contraction by saying, "I really shouldn't let them affect me." To unravel your nervous system, you must listen to what's true in your body at *this* moment. Don't try to override your current experience with what you think you should be feeling. If there's contraction, that's what you honor and release. Tell them what is okay and what is not for you. If they cannot respect your needs (because they're unable or unwilling), then you can remove yourself from the situation. It doesn't matter if they're trying their very best if their best is still not respecting what is okay and not okay for you.

Do not abandon yourself in order to keep someone else in their comfort zone.

Sometimes stepping away from a relationship creates space for something new to happen. You may choose to stay, but if it doesn't turn out the way you hope, just remember that *you* chose every step of the way to stay. Nothing is "happening *to* you." You're co-creating this by choosing to stay.

The good news is, there's no way to do this work and not learn to respect your needs. You may take a step back from a friendship, set limits on how often you see family, maybe require one non-family member present to keep a family member on best behavior, or maybe you end a relationship. Keep feeling through any contraction that arises and feel it fully into expansion. Also, feel free to give them a copy of this book!

When you've stabilized expansion in your system, and it's your natural default state, you'll be stronger in your ability to handle others' judgments. People are not trying to hurt you; they're just protecting their sense of self, their worldview, and keeping themselves safe in their comfort zone. Even knowing that, it may still hurt, and you may feel misunderstood, unseen, and even alone for a while. Keep doing the work, and once you've stabilized expansion, you'll have embodied openness, acceptance, and understanding. It won't just be your mind telling you, "I should understand it's not about me." Your body will actually feel free of the charge, the hurt, the contraction.

Who are your freedom friends? Make a list of all your friendships and categorize them by 1) friendships you'd like to grow, 2) friendships you'd like to maintain, and 3) friendships you're ready to release. This is a live document, with these relationships dynamically moving in and out of your categories organically. You'll want to revisit this list regularly to see what changes you'd like to make.

SIGNS YOU'RE EXPANDING

When you expand, you'll notice the things that used to bother you and create contraction don't seem to bother you as much anymore. Things that used to scare or worry you don't anymore. You feel progressively more relaxed in your being. Past insecurities, embarrassments, or shame will no longer hold power over you. Even with the things you used to be scared were true about you, you'll embody this knowledge:

"There is a part of me that can be this way at times and I'm okay with that. I accept *all* of me."

In expansion, you no longer reject any parts of you. You acknowledge and integrate them so that they don't unconsciously own you. De-weaponize all those things that are so triggering to you because there is a part of you that can be that way at times. You don't have to judge the hell out of it in yourself or in others. In expansion, you can accept all your parts—flaws, imperfections, messiness, fears, and insecurities. You will no longer need people to see you a certain way which frees you from caring about what others think. Nothing you accept about yourself will put you into contraction. All characteristics are welcome in balance. It would've evolved out of existence otherwise. Imbalance comes from staying in contraction, with a tight bandwidth on reality. In expansion, you're big enough to hold all your parts with no judgment of any of them and mastery over all of them.

POP QUIZ: DO THE FOLLOWING CREATE CONTRACTION OR EXPANSION?

Without knowing anything else about the persons who said each of these statements, what is your sense for the quality of life each one is living based merely on the level of consciousness of these statements? Circle C if you think they are living in Contraction or E if they seem to be in Expansion.

1. "I am single and really want to find my soulmate. Every time I go out, I'm hoping to meet my person." C   E

2. "I have to be #1 at whatever I do, I need to be the very best. I must win." C   E

3. "I really want to have a baby and have been trying for years. I don't know what I'll do if I can't get pregnant." C   E

4. "I love my partner and feel so grateful to have our relationship. I hope it lasts forever, but even if it doesn't, to have felt this way at all in my life is everything." C   E

5. "I hope my partner doesn't find anyone they want to be with more than me, even the thought of it breaks my heart." C   E

6. "I don't know what the right move is. What if I make the wrong decision and we fail? We'd lose everything." C   E

7. "I'm going to go for it and start my own company. It may fail, but I know I can always go back to working for someone again if I need to." C   E

8. "I would love it to go exactly how I want, and I'm leaving room for it to be different from what I envision." C   E

9. "I don't see it your way, but I can understand why we see it differently. How can we move forward now that we understand we may not agree?" C   E

10. How am I? My car broke down and I lost my job,   C   E
    how do you think I am?

11. "I got dumped and I lost my job. This is the most   C   E
    uncertainty I've ever been in. I feel powerless and
    scared. I'm doing my best to hold the vision for
    something better to come."

12. "It didn't turn out the way I hoped it would, but   C   E
    somehow I trust that things will work."

13. "I can't believe I just went for it. I was so scared   C   E
    to embarrass myself, but I just went for it
    anyway and I feel amazing, like I saw what I was
    made of!"

Do any of these statements sound like something you would say?
Notice the ones that put you into contraction and see how you
can recalibrate. If you're not ready to flip the script 180 degrees,
(because your nervous system cannot accept that possibility yet),
go for a 90-degree difference.

Here are the Contraction statements shifted 90 degrees toward
Expansion:
1. "I am single and really want to find my soulmate. Every time I
   go out, I'm hoping to meet my person."
   90-degree shift: "I'd love to meet my person. I trust that I'll
   find them soon."
2. "I have to be #1 at whatever I do, I need to be the very best. I
   must win."
   90-degree shift: "I love winning. It's fun for me, and I'll
   always try to, but you win some and you lose some."
3. "I really want to have a baby and have been trying for years. I
   don't know what I'll do if I can't get pregnant."
   90-degree shift: "I would really love to have a baby. I trust
   it'll happen soon. If I can't get pregnant, I'll explore other
   options."

4. "I hope my partner doesn't find anyone they want to be with more than me, even the thought of it breaks my heart."

   90-degree shift: "I love my partner so much and I believe they feel the same way about me. I'm glad we found each other."

5. "I don't know what the right move is. What if I make the wrong decision and we fail? We'd lose everything."

   90-degree shift: "I don't know what the right decision is. I'm going to gather more information and make the best call. I'll also think of a plan B and C in case we need them."

6. "How am I? My car broke down and I lost my job, how do you think I am?"

   90-degree shift: "How am I? My car broke down and I lost my job. Honestly, it feels really shitty right now. I'm updating my resume and going to see if I can get a loan to fix my car."

The actions you take from expansion versus contraction will make all the difference. *You decide.*

YOUR NEW MUSE

Practice the tools in this book. Keep doing things that feel expansive at a 10 for you. What is a 10 for you will be different from what is a 10 for others. Trust and follow expansion in *your* body. Become so in tune with yourself that you can discern what creates expansion for you and choose that. Practice feeling as often as you can as if you're building a new muscle. Release anything that is in the way of expansion: old beliefs, relationships, a job, or obligations. In any moment, ask, "Do I feel expanded or contracted right now?" "Is this thought creating momentum for expansion or contraction?"

Pay attention to how you feel.

Does this belief about how to make money make you feel contracted or expanded?

Notice the shows, TV programs, and movies you watch. Do they put you into contraction or expansion?

Do you watch scary movies that keep you on edge? Yes, I know some people love them, and if you want to go to the contraction gym and lift contraction weights, that's what you're doing, letting your nervous system build up contraction.

Notice the food you eat.

Notice how you felt in that conversation.

Notice how you feel in this room.

Does interacting with this person make you feel contracted or expanded?

Does your work make you feel contracted or expanded?

Notice how you talk to yourself, your judgments, opinions, comparisons.

Ask, *does this expand me or contract me?*

If you feel contraction, get curious and go into it, turn it up to 100 percent, and fully feel what's there. Relax into the discomfort and accept and allow what is present. Give your nervous system the repetition of feeling safe to feel whatever arises. Relax your nervous system so you can sensitize your body to feel what it's telling you. Listen for the wisdom that every emotion carries.

Until you feel and release your contractions, your contractive lens will continue bringing in its expected circumstances because perception becomes reality. The patterns of contraction in your nervous system will attract its matching puzzle piece. You'll find yourself in endless reenactments of familiar loops. People who touch your wounds will continue entering your life. Circumstances that create fear, anger, guilt, and shame will keep happening until you alchemize those contractions. Reality appears to keep bringing you the same lessons until you learn them.

I challenge you to go where you don't want to go. The discomfort in these places will cause separation, disconnection, and contraction until you release it. Go to where the discomfort is the worst and turn it up to 100 percent. Accept and allow this intensity, and then follow it by asking yourself, *What's here now?* Continue breathing through all that arises, allowing all the sensations and emotions to flow through, until the contraction dissipates and you're left in an empty, blissful state of expansion. You will feel emptiness and everythingness at the same time, merged with spaceless, timeless nothingness. You've entered the zero-point field, the field of infinite possibilities and probabilities. From here, you can bend reality.

Remember, suffering is pulling away from feeling what's in the present moment, while expansion comes from allowing yourself to feel it all. Continue transmuting any area of contraction (limiting beliefs, memories, anger, hurt, anxiety, pain, sadness, fear, disappointment) into expansion. This is about developing a brand-new relationship with discomfort.

I've seen Qigong Masters ask new students to hold a squat (the horse stance) for 10 minutes, breathing, smiling, and finding a way to enjoy the feeling of discomfort. This is another way to rewire your brain and develop a new relationship to discomfort. Your relationship with discomfort is the *most powerful relationship you can cultivate.* Do you tap out, avoid, suppress, repress, numb, push through it, try to "overcome" it, or get it over with as fast as you can—or can you sit with it? Can you rest in it, relax there, go into it, feel safe with it, even turn it up, and feel it flow through you, leaving you in expansion?

I believe the reason Qigong has been taught for over 5,000 years is because it is an embodied practice of the concepts in this book. It was traditionally used by Chinese martial art practitioners to improve their fighting abilities. Through breath and movement, you bring this knowledge into the body, feeling what it's like to be grounded, strong, and solid while in expansion. Instead of gripping, bracing, and holding your body in defense (the traditional contraction of fight/flight ready), you firmly plant your feet into the ground, feeling rooted and open at the same time. When I practice Qigong, I feel the rewiring of masculine precision and structure with feminine flow and fluidity. I move from positions of contraction right into movements of expansion.

Through the movements, I can literally feel the vulnerability of my heart—that fluttering sensation of feeling unguarded—not sure I feel safe being this open and undefended. Then I combine that with a movement that is solid and grounded, and it feels like *"I got this"* in my body. I train my nervous system to feel new states of undefended power. *This is what sovereignty feels like in my body.* I'm neither flimsy and porous with no boundaries (which we sometimes associate with going with the flow), nor am I ready to fight or defend myself (rigid and tight in contraction). I'm in a solid, powerful state of expansion. My body and nervous system get reps of feeling safe in vulnerability, safe in discomfort, even powerful in them. Its original name "Dao-Yin" means "leading and guiding energy." Releasing contraction and accessing expansion is the way of letting qi (life force energy) flow. Qigong Masters have been tapped into this for thousands of years.

The only way to access greater states of expansion is by feeling through contraction. Release it out of your body. Otherwise, you're merely avoiding contraction and calling that expansion. It's not about avoiding pain or doing what feels safe to avoid contraction. It's about doing what is a 10 for you and feeling through the fear that comes up as you stretch beyond your comfort zone.

If you're feeling expansive or even neutral, ask yourself, *What would feel more expansive right now?* and do that. Surround yourself with people, projects, activities, books, food, support, and environments that feel like a 10. As you do this, and drop things that aren't a 10, your baseline of expansion will jump an octave, and whatever is still creating contraction will become crystal clear.

Once you drop a contraction anchor (relationship, job, environment, core belief), everything else that was causing contraction that you didn't notice as much before because you were used to a baseline of contraction will become obvious to you. All of this gets to go too. When you're in contraction, you'll find reasons for why you're in contraction:

"Because I'm stressed with work."

"Because I'm worried about our kids."

"Because my partner is upset."

"Because our bills went up."

"Because I'm out of shape."

"Because we're not having sex."

"Because I need a vacation."

You'll find endless reasons to keep feeling contracted.

When you've conditioned your nervous system to feel expanded, it will feel obvious, like a jolt, when you feel contracted. As you release fear, guilt, shame, contraction, you'll be catapulted into expansion which will energize you beyond anything you've felt before. You'll give birth to new ideas, be an open channel for inspiration, and your joy will come from how well you cultivate expansion.

One vision that I have for you is that over time, not only will you accept and allow your emotions without judgment, but you will also learn to trust and *love* them. Instead of running from contraction, you accept and embrace it. Let contraction become *your muse.*

My hope for you is that you'll become as excited as I do to reclaim your power by fully feeling contraction, knowing that every trigger of hurt, anger, judgment, fear, shame, or guilt is just showing you where you don't feel safe—where you can more fully love and accept yourself. Embody the knowing that contraction comes from pulling away from the present moment and expansion comes from feeling whatever arises. Your body will no longer feel resistant or unsafe toward contraction but will relax into fully feeling it and enjoying the ride into expansion. One client recently shared that when he used to notice discomfort, he'd try to do something to get out of the feeling. Sometimes he'd meditate or do breathwork, other times he'd call someone, drink, or smoke. Now when he notices any emotions, he says, "This is a big opportunity I can't miss!"

I invite you to role model the freedom that comes from feeling your emotions. If you feel inspired to be a part of this movement, share an Emotions Selfie with #FeelingMyself.

EXPANSION EVOLVES

What you find expansive will change and elevate as you expand. At first, the idea of having a certain amount of money will feel expansive, then maybe finding love, then creating a vision you want, then impacting the world. What you want will evolve until it's aligned with your highest self. Who knows what the expanded version of you will want next? When you make cultivating expansion a part of your daily practice (feeling, thinking, receiving, and giving from a place of expansion), you boost your immune system, and begin to understand that the more you feel expansive, the more expanded you become. From here you can change the world *if that would make you feel expansive.*

As you've read this book, each chapter has upgraded your lens on reality. You are not the same person who opened it. Your bandwidth has increased and your nervous system has expanded so what you can take in (the connections you're able to make, how deep this information lands) is also evolving. If you reread this book, because you are expanded, what you'll get out of reading the same content will also expand. Depending on where your consciousness was when you found this book, you may have absorbed 90 to 100 percent of it on your first read, or you may have absorbed 5 to 10 percent. Wherever you are is perfect. You will embody more each time you read it.

I expanded the week this book wrote me. I embodied and stabilized a new level of expansion every day and night as my nervous system entrained to the universal truths I'm sharing here. I continue to read this book regularly myself and I am expanding each time I read it.

It's a funny place to be because I can still remember how it felt to be the version of me before this book. It's super fresh. I can empathize with all the struggles of making the transition. I remember what it was like to experience fears, insecurities, and attachments. I remember what it felt like to allow my mind to complicate things. I remember how it felt to negotiate with myself, rationalize my decisions, and assume that reality fit into my understanding of it. I took my understanding of it all so seriously and was sucked into making everything way more important than any of it actually is. There was a drama to life, and an enjoyment of feeling as if I were on a quest.

When I started my journey of expansion, I did not know what would be revealed or who I would become. This path led to my rewilding. For me, rewilding means finding all the places I've been conditioned to domesticate myself.[58] Where have I numbed my senses, lost touch with my intuition and instincts? Where have I ignored my own sight? Where have I edited my expression to be normal, polished, and intellectual? Where have I toned down my sensuality, pleasure, and aliveness? Where have I let the details of daily life tame my life force? Where have I clipped my dreams? Where do I go along with things that I'm not enthusiastic about? Where do I dismiss, rationalize, and gloss over my feelings? The last decade has been about giving myself full permission to live in *every* way. To be wild and free from my own and others' expectations. To explore *all* my edges. To shine all my facets. To stand sovereign in my sacred nature. To be crazy in love with life and follow my expansion.

Before releasing my contractions, I was going after my dreams with both the gas pedal and brake pedal engaged at the same time. I went from climbing a mountain in contraction to enjoying quantum leaps in expansion. Today there's no emotion that I can't or won't be with so I can live and operate from higher levels of expansion. I follow my bliss, pleasure, play, and purpose. By living in expansion, I have the freedom to choose only the work I love to do, with clients who feel like a 10 for me. I earn the value of the impact of my work. I have the freedom to live and work from any location. I consciously cultivate relationships that feel expansive and release all that are not. I have freedom from the contraction of living with limiting beliefs and only choose supportive ones. I consciously consume food, books, entertainment, and experiences that feel like a 10 for me. I can embrace all of this because I have complete emotional freedom.

That's what I want for you.

Today I'm resting in a new, unfamiliar place that's hard to explain, even to my romantic partner. I now like things I didn't like before. I now don't care for things I used to love. I feel both unattached to all that is in this life (including friends, family, and relationships) as well as the most profound gratitude and love I've ever felt for it all, and the deepest desire to serve. I know there's no end state to expansion so I can't anticipate what the new version of me will feel like tomorrow.

Peter S. Beagle said, "Wisdom is finding joy in bewilderment."[59] Embrace the mystery of things you may know and things you may never know. Enjoy the journey of not knowing where you're going or who you're becoming, the bewilderment of your evolution. Trust the process of expansion, and what will be created through it. Your sense of identity may rapidly change. Know that any judgments or fears at the prospect of your expansion come only from this side of your consciousness. I've become a version of me that my previous self would've judged and been scared of, and yet on the other side, I'm freer and more fulfilled than I'd ever imagined was possible. I live in pure gratitude, excitement, and aliveness every single day, because *I let myself feel everything.*

Enjoy the journey of not knowing where you're going or who you're becoming, the bewilderment of your evolution.

EXERCISE: YOUR EVOLUTION

In what ways have you noticed yourself expand from reading this book? What beliefs did you hold at the start that have since shifted? What have you learned about yourself? What contraction anchors are you ready to release? Where are you craving expansion in your life?

CHAPTER 12
Make Your Own Map

NOW THAT WE'VE TALKED ABOUT YOUR MIND, emotions, and body, you may be wondering, *Is there a spirit?* Get yourself into expansion, and you'll be able to answer that question yourself. That may be my next book! This book is my expression of expansion. It expanded me as it wrote me. While the words will enter your mind, my intention is for this to be a transmission of expansion in your being. Some truths are meant to be felt, not told. May this book be your on-ramp into expansion.

I'm not asking you for faith in anything or anyone. Yet from what I've seen, it seems easier for humans to put faith and trust outside themselves in a god or in someone else who has the answers. The only trust or faith worth having is the one in yourself.

Before reading this book, you likely believed that trust is a vulnerable state, and control is an invulnerable state. You may have worried that trust leads to being taken advantage of, being hurt, looking stupid, or failing. However, now you see how the need to control puts us into contraction, makes us insecure, puts us into a tiny box of what is acceptable, and makes us vulnerable to anything not going the way we want it to go.

> **Here is your eleventh unlearning:** *Control is the vulnerable state. Trust is the invulnerable state.*

When we do not trust, we become impatient or pessimistic, and then take action from this place of contraction. I'm not suggesting you blindly trust. I'm inviting you to trust yourself, trust your feelings, and trust what you have access to in expansion. Trust that you can be with whatever discomfort arises. Trust that it's all meant to grow you. Trust that life is creating circumstances that offer your greatest opportunity for expansion in every moment. Trust that you have access to solutions not available to you in contraction. Watch how agile, creative, and antifragile you become. Trust is the invulnerable state. Trust is a prerequisite for expansion.

ENLIGHTENMENT

Enlightenment is not about changing who you are but, about recognizing who you are. You stop seeking anything as you've released all the old stories, wounds, and limiting beliefs that set you in motion seeking. You're deeply relaxed in your own skin. You naturally become present. It's no longer an elusive state that you try to achieve, but an extension of your new state of expansion.

Eckhart Tolle[60] and many spiritual teachers discuss the importance of being present. However, I don't believe you can tell someone to be present. You must become the expanded version of you, for whom being present comes naturally. Similarly, you may understand that seeking appears to be the root of suffering, but you cannot mentally will yourself to stop seeking either. Your unacceptance of your true nature makes you seek. Your avoidance of contraction causes you to seek. You can become the expanded version of you for whom *not seeking* is your natural state. Again, rather than memorize rules and ideals, and strive to be anything (merely another form of seeking), expand and all these rules and ideals will become embodied as your authentic self.

I've heard clients say, "But (doing or saying that) doesn't feel authentic to me." It's almost as if spiritual teachers have crossed over to another experience of reality and they're reporting back to you what's different over there, explaining:

- I'm present.
- I'm patient.
- I no longer take things personally.
- I am accepting and grateful.
- I feel self-love.
- My mind is still.
- I forgive easily.
- I no longer seek.
- I have faith that everything is happening in the best and highest of all.
- I communicate calmly.
- I feel one with everything.
- I value being over doing.
- I don't take myself too seriously.
- I feel connected to my inner child.
- I enjoy and appreciate every moment.
- I choose love over fear.
- I desire to serve others.
- I trust.
- I surrender.

But many spiritual teachers don't quite know how they got there. So they tell you:

- Be present.
- Don't take things personally.
- Be accepting and grateful.
- Love yourself.
- Still your mind.
- Stop seeking.
- Trust.
- Do less, *be* more.

You can mentally want this for yourself, but it will feel like an elusive ideal, something you need to remind yourself to do constantly and still struggle with or forget. Then seeking enlightenment becomes just another place you're not accepting where you are right now, judging yourself, and creating contraction. You may tell yourself:

- "Ah, I should feel more self-compassion."
- "I really need to be more present."
- "I really shouldn't take things so personally."

Then you've just replaced chasing money, beauty, and success with chasing enlightenment. This is a journey of unraveling and unlearning, not striving and fixing. Feel your contractions so you can release them and become your expanded self, the version of you for whom these ideals become your natural way of being. Reprogram your nervous system to expansion so you can live from there. Then the ideals will no longer live only in your mind but will have become embodied. What

When you have an idea, breathe life into it for your enjoyment.

you'll experience in expansion will be beyond your current mind's imagination. It's the difference between thinking you're a horse and trying to run faster (contraction) and realizing you have wings and flying (expansion).

Life is meant to be expansive. When you have an idea, breathe life into it for your enjoyment. Doing it for any other reason takes you out of expansion. Even "*I have to save the planet*" urgency is contraction. When we're in expansion, we co-create with *God*, when we're in contraction, we co-create with *Fear*.

You may go on countless medicine journeys, talk to angels, and connect to god through sex—just don't place your power outside of you. Be wary of coaches, teachers, or mentors who make you believe that the answers lie outside of you. Notice if a teacher empowers you to trust yourself or enjoys their power by making you believe *they* know better what's best for you. Watch out for anyone who validates any belief that you're broken, not whole, or that something's wrong and needs fixing. The answer is *not* outside of you. Our wiring to seek, strive, and fix leads us to contraction. *There is not one path.* Every individual has a different path. If you pay attention to how you feel, you'll be on yours.

I wrote this book to demystify it all for you. While many coaches and teachers are selling you their maps, I'm inviting you to create and follow your *own* map. Now that you understand the simplicity hidden behind the complexity, you can be your own mapmaker, and plot your own course. I have offered you the first principles behind growth, self-development, and real magic. You can take it from here.

THE LEVELS OF MOTIVATION

There are four levels of motivation for creating your own map to access expansion and your supernatural abilities. *Every level is incredible.*

Motivation Level 1: Feeling expanded feels good and I like feeling good. I'd like to live more of my days from here.

Motivation Level 2: When I feel good and expansive, everything is easier. I have more energy, more time, more creative flow, and people seem drawn to my magnetic personality. I'm more productive. Things feel smooth. There's a harmonious rhythm to my days. More feels possible from here.

Motivation Level 3: I'm so productive in expansion that I can actually get more done doing less. Things come easily. I feel luckier and experience more synchronicity. It's easier to trust that it's all working out for me. I'm happier, and less attached to any outcome. Nothing *has* to happen anymore. I know I'll be okay no matter what. I've naturally become more patient. I'm listening to my intuition, which is stronger. I feel grateful and fulfilled. My life has improved in ways I never thought was possible. I control less and trust more. This is a nice, new baseline.

Motivation Level 4: Holy shit! This is magic. Psychic perception, synchronicities, manifestation—*whoa*, I can do that? I created that simply by visioning it. I'm manifesting things left and right! Creating from nothing in no time at all. I didn't know I had this superpower. Did I always have that, or did I wake up with it? I'm receiving downloads all the time. This is *fun! What else can I do?* What else can happen that I never thought was possible? This is beyond my wildest imagination. I'm bending reality. I'm making quantum leaps monthly, weekly, daily! I'm FUCKING ALIVE!

When you get to Level 4, you may start to develop your own relationship to "spirituality," which for me is my relationship to the mystery of the unknown. It's how much curiosity, value, and respect I have for this mystery. For me, cultivating spirituality is not about praying or meditating. It's about cultivating expansion, which dictates how I show up in every moment. I experience a more magical dimension with access to supernatural downloads, abilities, and connection to the unseen and unknown mysteries. I develop senses beyond the five I already knew I had. Tapped in, you might start to wonder, *Is there a God? Aliens? Simulation? Will we ever know?*

You may say, "It doesn't matter! This is incredible. I wish everyone could play this game of life. I'm awake! I can do that? I had no idea. We *are* infinitely wise, powerful, and abundant!" You will continue to be amazed, but no longer surprised.

Congratulations! You've accessed your supernatural abilities. You took the red pill; you broke free from the system. Now enjoy the ride! Whatever level you decide to rest on, or however long you choose to stay on each level, or even what you decide to do with all your newfound abilities is perfect. Why do I say that? That's how you stay in expansion. Keep holding all of it lightly. Choose your own adventure. All missions are equal. Choose one that's fun for you. There's no "better"; thinking so only creates contraction.

You're never done expanding, and there is no wrong or right level. Now at least you have the choice. The choice you maybe didn't realize you had before reading this book. No matter what you choose, you are magic. I know what you're capable of. I can't wait for you to experience *you*!

You've seen the five codes to bending reality throughout this book. Let's look at them together.

CODES TO BENDING REALITY

1. *Recognize where you are: "Am I contracted or expanded right now?"*
2. *Choose your thoughts carefully.*
3. *Feel whatever arises.*
4. *Be in expansion while you reach for more.*
5. *Feel your vision coming true from a place of expansion.*

These codes allow you to release contraction and access expansion so you can bend reality.

It's *simple* but *not easy* because it requires eleven key unlearnings.

1. *The moment we seek to be a certain way, think a certain way, do a certain thing, and are not comfortable just the way we are—in our own unique expression of life—we create contraction.*
2. *As soon as you relate to anything in your life as "must make something happen," you're in contraction.*
3. *Almost all of your actions, thoughts, decisions, emotions, and behaviors come from the programming of your subconscious.*
4. *All emotions are simply energy-in-motion, which is why you cannot selectively numb "negative" emotions and feel only "positive" emotions.*
5. *There are many things you can do, but the thing that's going to get you access to your supernatural abilities is the thing that feels like play for you because that's what gives you access to expansion.*
6. *The way to remove contraction in your body is to go into the eye of the storm, and fully feel it.*

7. *If you don't feel your emotions, then the energy patterns get stuck and metastasize, creating dis-ease in the body, which becomes disease.*
8. *If you only focus on expansion, you are bypassing what needs to be seen and capping your upper limits on expansion. If you're just focused on removing contraction, you miss what's possible when you entrain your nervous system to expansion. Combining the two is where the magic happens.*
9. *It's not until we admit to ourselves how much pain we're in that we can access sufficient energy to say, "Enough!" and create a new reality.*
10. *You can't manifest anything you want from contraction.*
11. *Control is the vulnerable state. Trust is the invulnerable state.*

You are the one you've been waiting for. If you choose to bring on a guide for your journey, find a guide who shows you how powerful *you* are, not how powerful they are. While many can share a message, few truly embody the message. Find those whose life shows they *know* it.

Follow expansion and you'll become the most expanded version of you, your freest, truest self, with your own unique supernatural access. The greatest gift you can give this planet is your connection to your expanded self. Listen to *how you feel* to come home to who you truly are.

EXERCISE: PLOT YOUR COURSE

Which level of motivation do you find yourself on? How much curiosity, value, and respect do you have for the mystery of the unknown? How expanded do you feel right now?

Consider the following key areas of your life: Health, Romantic Relationship, Career, Lifestyle, Family, Money, Time, Mission, Community, and Hobbies. Rate these areas on a scale of 1 to 10 (where 1 is a nightmare and 10 is the dream) and explain why you chose that rating. If this area of your life were a 10, what would it look like? Describe it in detail. What actions can you take today to move you toward a 10 in each of these areas?

CONCLUSION
The Ecstasy of Coming Home

I'D LOVE TO SEAL THIS BOOK WITH ONE OF MY POEMS called "The Ecstasy of Coming Home" that came to me at the completion of writing it. One of the unexpected joys of this journey is spontaneous creation.

> We are all magicians
> writing spells into every message
> whether a tweet or a book
> We infuse into every creation
> food, text, sound, or look,
> The energy of magic
>
> The thing itself is neutral
> It's what we infuse into the thing
> with our human spirit's intention
> that either nourishes or poisons
>
> Art is one expression of spirit's intention
> Judgment is another

This is what it means to say we are creators
powerful beyond measure

I am an Oracle
My heart and mind come together to express with more accuracy in
transmission
than what three-dimensions can handle
My form of communication creates portals
Tears down the wall of Truman Show reality

Trust my word
Trust my voice
Trust my sight

I am an Artist
And every sense: taste, touch, sound, scent, sight
Every tool: mind, heart, and body
is my paintbrush
Human experience is my canvas

Poetry and song is one way to bring back beauty
to what has made people jaded to the truths the heart already knows
It finds "new ways" to tell the same truths
Dressed in some layers, some colors, some sounds
but they are the same truths

Every artist brings to life
truths older than time
We remember together
The planet, God, Soul of the adventure is healing
By remembering through each of us

Humans are taking longer and longer to remember
If we had no memory, there would be no time
Time is not running out, we are just getting better at forgetting

We know when we are born
By the time we learn how to do this human thing called life
We forget

The artists, dreamers, visionaries remember

We all just want to feel again
Feel richly, feel moved, the way we feel as babies
About anything at all

Love is one of the last places we let ourselves truly feel —
Feel everything
Every last tear, every last hope, every last longing
But even love is being lost

Like the last petal in the Beast's magical rose
We must save love
The last place we allow ourselves to go to remember
What it feels like to feel

I am (<u>state your name</u>*), one who remembers...*
—*Victoria Song*

I can't wait for you to experience how powerful you are.

Your Alchemist,
Victoria

P.S. Do you feel more expanded after reading this book? Wait till you read it again!

I invite you to continue this journey of expansion with me, the wild unknowing and delight of what is yet to be created. I'm always releasing new offerings from the edge of my own becoming which you can find on my website: www.victoriasong.me

Thank You

THESE CODES ARE NOT OWNED OR CREATED BY ANYONE. This ancient wisdom flows from many sources. I am sharing it in a modern context to make this esoteric knowledge accessible to a wider audience.

In these uncertain and chaotic times, now more than ever, we need to learn how to relax our nervous systems so that we are not manipulated into binary thinking and viewpoints around politics, race, class, gender, sexuality, nationality, or faith. My hope is that we learn how to break free from the matrix of fear programming and wake up from the sleepy indifference, boredom, and compromise most the planet is living in. May you learn to honor your heart: love fiercely, feel deeply, listen for your heart's truths, and follow its desires. My hope is that we use the codes to bending reality to experience true fulfillment no matter what life brings us so we can create a life and world we love.

I'm thankful to all my teachers, and the lineage of teachers before them with special thanks to David Mehler, Alex Moscow, Jennifer Hudye, Wendy Gutin, and Ally Bogard. Connecting the dots by seeing themes in multiple places lit up the whole picture that became this book.

I'm grateful for every client who has trusted me on their journey and whose results gave me the courage and confidence to share this book with the world. I'm grateful to every person and circumstance in my life including exes, bullies, classmates, colleagues, friends, and family. In fact, I'm grateful to the ones who co-created the hardest experiences of my life because you gave me the greatest opportunities to reclaim the most amount of power. You helped me remember *who I am* and *why I'm here*, and for that I send nothing but gratitude to you on your path.

I'm grateful for every wound, valley, every initiation that has sculpted me into the woman I am today. There is nothing our missions require of us that we cannot handle. Every hard thing in my life has taught me how to alchemize pain into power, contraction into expansion. Thank you, Life. Thank you for always giving me exactly what I need.

Deepest gratitude to my greatest soul sponsor, James Dougherty, thank you for co-creating a safe, accepting space to explore and release our contractions, and stand for each other's greatest expansion.

I'm turning 33 years old as I write this and hope to live as long as possible, so I can contribute as much as I can. I'm grateful to live every day fully alive in expansion, knowing that one day, I'll get to say, "Boy did I LIVE, Boy did I LOVE, boy did I SERVE, boy did I STRETCH, boy did I have FUN, boy did I SHINE. Onward."

Endnotes

1. Brené Brown, *Dare to Lead* Training Program, September 2019, https://daretolead.brenebrown.com/.
2. Ellie Lisitsa, "The Four Horsemen: Criticism, Contempt, Defensiveness, and Stonewalling," The Gottman Institute, April 23, 2013, https://www.gottman.com/blog/the-four-horsemen-recognizing-criticism-contempt-defensiveness-and-stonewalling/.
3. The Albert Team, "Positive and Negative Feedback Loops in Biology," Albert (website), June 1, 2020, https://www.albert.io/blog/positive-negative-feedback-loops-biology/.
4. Geoff MacDonald and Mark Leary, "Why Does Social Exclusion Hurt? The Relationship Between Social and Physical Pain," *Psychological Bulletin* 131, no. 2 (April 2005): 202–223, https://www.researchgate.net/publication/7994338_Why_Does_Social_Exclusion_Hurt_The_Relationship_Between_Social_and_Physical_Pain#:~:text=MacDonald%20and%20Leary%20(2005)%20conducted,experienced%20as%20painful%20because%20%22reactions.
5. Mark Twain, *Adventures of Tom Sawyer* (The Heritage Press, 2000).
6. Emma Young in *New Scientist* magazine, October 9, 2018.
7. Richard Rudd, *Gene Keys: Embracing Your Higher Purpose* (Watkins, 2015).

8. Brené Brown, "Listening to Shame," TED Talk, March 16, 2012, https://www.ted.com/talks/brene_brown_listening_to_shame?language=en.

9. Brené Brown, "Shame vs. Guilt," Brené Brown (blog), January 14, 2013, https://brenebrown.com/blog/2013/01/14/shame-v-guilt/.

10. Stephen B. Karpman, *A Game Free Life* (Drama Triangle Publications, 2020).

11. Julia Cameron, Artist's Way (Jeremy P. Tarcher/Perigee, 1992).

12. NaniLea Diamond, Full Glory Live, accessed April 15, 2021, https://www.nanileadiamond.com/home.

13. "About Us," Somatic Experiencing Trauma International (website), accessed April 14, 2021, https://traumahealing.org/about-us/.

14. Diamond, Full Glory Live.

15. Lauren Landry, "Why Emotional Intelligence Is Important in Leadership," *Harvard Business Review*, April 3, 2019, https://online.hbs.edu/blog/post/emotional-intelligence-in-leadership.

16. Inspired by author's work with NaniLea Diamond.

17. Matt Kahn, *Whatever Arises, Love That: A Revolution that Begins with You* (audiobook), (Sounds True, 2016).

18. Rudd, *Gene Keys*.

19. Rudd, *Gene Keys*.

20. Kahn, *Whatever Arises*.

21. Catherine Price, "Putting Down Your Phone May Help You Live Longer," *New York Times*, April 24, 2019, https://www.nytimes.com/2019/04/24/well/mind/putting-down-your-phone-may-help-you-live-longer.html.

22. Price, "Putting Down Your Phone."

23. Shane Parrish, "Sheila Heen: Decoding Difficult Conversations," Knowledge Project Podcast, episode #57, accessed April 14, 2021, https://fs.blog/knowledge-project/.

24. Parrish, "Sheila Heen."

25. Antonio Demasio, *Descartes' Error: Emotion, Reason, and the Human Brain* (Penguin, 1994).

26. Albert Mehrabian, *Nonverbal Communication* (Routledge, 2007).

27. "Co-Active Is the New Language of Leadership," Co-Active Training Institute, accessed April 15, 2021, https://coactive.com/.

28. Kyle Cease, "Evolving Out Loud," Dolby Theatre performance.

29. Steve Jobs, "'You've Got to Find What You Love' Jobs Says" (Stanford Commencement Speech), Stanford News, June 14, 2005, https://news.stanford.edu/2005/06/14/jobs-061505/.

30. "Co-Active Is the New Language of Leadership."

31. Henry Ford, *My Life and Work* (Garden City Publishing, 1922).

32. "What Is the Placebo Effect?," WebMD, February 8, 2020, https://www.webmd.com/pain-management/what-is-the-placebo-effect.

33. Johann Hari, *Lost Connections: Uncovering the Real Causes of Depression—and the Unexpected Solutions* (Bloomsbury Publishing, 2019).

34. Rhonda Byrne, *The Secret* (Atria Books, 2006).

35. Benjamin Radford and Mary Carmichael, "Special Report: Secrets and Lies," *Skeptical Inquirer*, March 29, 2007.

36. Robert A. Scheinfeld, *Busting Loose from the Money Game: Mind-Blowing Strategies for Changing the Rules of a Game You Can't Win* (Wiley, 2006).

37. Dr. Joe Dispenza, *Becoming Supernatural: How Common People Are Doing the Uncommon* (Hay House Inc., 2019).

38. Philip B. Clarke et al., "The Straight Path to Healing: Using Motivational Interviewing to Address Spiritual Bypass," Journal of Counseling & Development 91, no. 1 (January 2013): 87-94, https://onlinelibrary.wiley.com/doi/abs/10.1002/j.1556-6676.2013.00075.x.

39. Charles B. Ferster and B. F. Skinner, *Schedules of Reinforcement* (Appleton-Century-Crofts, 1957).

40. Cease, "Evolving Out Loud."

41. Learned from author's work with NaniLea Diamond.

42. Homepage, Strozzi Institute, accessed April 15, 2021, https://strozziinstitute.com/.

43. Jobs, "'You've Got to Find What You Love.'"

44. Meredith Hart, "The 100 Most Famous Quotes of All Time," Hubspot, accessed April 15, 2021, https://blog.hubspot.com/sales/famous-quotes.

45. Hart, "The 100 Most Famous Quotes."

46. Hart, "The 100 Most Famous Quotes."

47. Hart, "The 100 Most Famous Quotes."

48. Caroline Myss, *Energy Anatomy* (audiobook) (Sounds True, 2001).

49. Inspired by author's work with NaniLea Diamond.

50. Karpman, *A Game Free Life*.

51. Learned from, Rudd, *Gene Keys*.

52. Paraphrased, Rudd, *Gene Keys.*

53. Diamond, Full Glory Live.

54. Learned from, Cease, "Evolving Out Loud."

55. See Lisitsa, "The Four Horsemen."

56. Inspired by author's work with NaniLea Diamond.

57. Inspired by author's work with NaniLea Diamond.

58. Inspired by author's work with NaniLea Diamond.

59. Peter S. Beagle, *We Never Talk about My Brother* (Tachyon Publications, 2009).

60. Homepage, Eckhart Tolle (website), accessed April 15, 2021, https://eckharttolle.com/.